SORTED!

SORTED!

ESSENTIAL SYSTEMS FOR
SUCCESSFUL SMALL BUSINESSES

BY

ALICE JENNINGS

First published in Great Britain by Practical Inspiration Publishing, 2019

ISBN 978-1-78860-099-6 (print)
    978-1-78860-096-5 (mobi)
    978-1-78860-097-2 (epub)

Practical Inspiration
PUBLISHING

Contents

In the beginning

How to get the most from this book

Most people pick up a book like this because they want to make changes. I know I do, and I also know how easy it is read an inspiring book that leaves me feeling like I need an extra month in the year just to get started with the ideas that are then buzzing around my head.

It is so easy to get sucked in by some great ideas only to find yourself quickly overwhelmed. Suddenly it stops feeling like a great way to transform your business and starts to feel like a huge mountain to climb while wearing stilettos, and it's much easier to grab a pack of Hobnobs and have a quick scroll through Instagram to get over it. Phew.

I don't want this to happen to you so please, please follow these guidelines:

1. Be realistic

If you only have a spare two hours a week you are not going to get very far trying to do something from every chapter. Start by picking a couple of easy to action 'quick wins' to buy you a little extra time and then use that time to take further actions towards your goals and see how that goes.

Every time you complete something you will feel like a productivity ninja, which will give you a boost and help you to get on the next step towards a business that is super slick. Then pick the next small step and repeat. The small steps will add up and before you know it, you'll be fully systemised and without the horrible feeling of over-whelm.

2. Be committed

I really wish that the mere act of reading this book could give you a super-slick business. Sadly, it can't. This is because systems are like Zumba.

When my first child was a few months old, I bought a Zumba CD. I was excited about dancing around the lounge reclaiming my pre-baby body. Unfortunately, it didn't work. I didn't do the work; the DVD is gathering dust next to the TV and I have a distinctly bubble-wrapped six pack.

Does this mean that Zumba doesn't help you to reclaim your pre-baby body? No. It means that I didn't do the work. System stuff is very similar. Does it work? Yes, but *only* if you do the work. It really doesn't matter how little time you feel you have to commit. Half an hour a week is a great start. It adds up to 26 hours a year, or more than three working days. Could you make changes in your business that would have a positive impact if you stopped everything else and focused for three days? You bet you could.

3. Be kind

It's easy to be a bad boss when you work for yourself. People who were perfectly lovely bosses in previous roles become the boss from hell when they are working for themselves. Do any of these seem familiar:

- Working ridiculous hours?
- Regularly working at weekends?
- Not paying yourself?
- No lunch breaks?
- No pension?
- No proper holidays (without email checking!)?
- No training?
- No bonuses or perks to speak of?

It's common to see small business owners treating themselves like this, striving to build the best business they can. Often it has completely the opposite effect, resulting in underperformance because of tiredness and lack of balance.

Try to structure the systems in your business so that they reward you for the hard work and effort that you put in. If you get a new client, give yourself a £20 cash bonus to spend on something frivolous. If you do your accounts for the month on time, then go for a walk in your favourite spot as a reward.

Working for yourself is a privilege and many of us don't make the most of it, getting stuck in the ways of employment that we learnt in a corporate role. If you want to walk your dog three times a day then make that a fixture in your diary so that you don't plan other things in. And if you don't make it happen, then be kind and try again the next day.

Systems vs tools

Throughout this book I will be talking about systems and tools. There are many ways to define both of these words but for the purposes of this book I will be talking about them like this:

- A *system*: a way of doing something, a series of steps that you take to get to an outcome.

- A *tool*: a piece of software or equipment that you use to get something done.

A *tool* could be a computer or piece of software, but without the *system* which defines how it works it's just an object. Think of a kettle: making a cup of tea requires a 'system' of getting cups and teabags and boiling the kettle. The kettle itself is just a 'tool' within that system and could, if required, be replaced by a pan of boiling water or an urn. The outcome remains the same even though different tools can be used.

How to use this book

There are two ways to use this book.

1. To solve a specific problem

If you just want to know about a specific type of system or technology then check out the contents and skip straight to that section. Each chapter is designed to work alone and give you an idea of your options.

2. To help you plan your ideal business and then carry out the steps required to get there

While targeting a problem in a specific area of your business can take the pressure off for a short time, you will get best results if you look at your business as a whole.

This is how I help my one-to-one clients; we start by looking at their business and I help them to choose the best systems for their business. Realising that not everyone has the resources to work with me individually, this book has translated that service into a book, with worksheets. By completing the exercises and making the choices at the end of each chapter, you will be able to develop an action plan for your business which will enable you to systemise like a ninja!

Right, let's get started.

Chapter 1
Getting started

Please adopt this mantra:

> I know best for my business

Starting a business is a bit like having a baby. Terrifying and exhilarating at the same time. The start of something new, and suddenly it feels like everyone thinks they can give you unsolicited advice.

You may not have had a baby but if you are reading this book you are probably thinking of starting, or have already started, your business. Fantastic news! And congratulations.

If there is one thing you take from this book then I hope it is this…

> …you are the very best person to make decisions for your business

No one else has the deep understanding of your hopes and goals for it, the way it makes you feel when you get up in the morning or when it keeps you awake at night. You, like 'mother', know best.

However, you are only able to make the best decision for your business if you have the correct information to enable you to choose from the many options out there, and pick the very specific combination of systems, tools and technologies that are right for your business, budget and your personal style.

It's so easy to meet someone who has tried a particular website designer or software tool that gave them great results and be persuaded that if you do just what they did then you will get great results also. But this is the same as suggesting that the diet that worked brilliantly for your friend will also work for you, or that your perfect house is also your brother's perfect house. Different things work for different people.

As you work through this book I will share the key systems and tools that a small business can use. Note that I say *can*, not *should*, because some of these will be relevant for you and some will not. And that's just fine!

What I hope is that you can make a clear choice about all the things I share and be able to allocate them to one of three categories:

- something you should definitely try
- something that may work for you in the future
- something that is just not relevant.

Then you can get on with doing the real work of growing your business and doing the work you love.

At the end of each chapter is a worksheet with a summary and checklist. These are also available to download and print out from my website: www.alicejennings. co.uk/book-bonuses

The worksheets challenge you to think about your business and decide whether any of the systems I talk about in that chapter could bring value to your business. It also asks you to prioritise the system depending on how much you could use it right now vs in one year or in three years, based on your plans for your business.

By completing the worksheet for each chapter, you will end up with a list of actions that you would like to take for your business, each with a priority. At the end of the book we will look at how you can turn this into a clear plan and if you choose, use a system to help you manage to make it into a reality.

If you carry out the plans then your business will be efficient; you will save time and money. In a nutshell, you will be SORTED!

Action: Download the worksheets from www.alicejennings.co.uk/book-bonuses

The SORTED Framework

I'm on a mission... to help small business owners find the right systems and technology to save them time and money.

I've been on this mission for a few years now and it has led me to create the SORTED Framework. Once you have identified your spot in the framework it enables you to defend yourself against well-intentioned advice and over-zealous salespeople, and to work out what systems and technology are appropriate for your business right now.

It's pretty simple (as all the best ideas tend to be) and I'd like to share it with you now. So without further ado I present.... (drum roll please):

The SORTED Framework

The SORTED Framework is based on two simple rules and is designed to help you identify what systems and technology are appropriate for your business right now. The two rules are:

Rule 1.   All businesses have (at least) three departments

Rule 2.   There are three stages of business

Let me explain a little more:

Rule 1. All businesses have three departments

Many of my clients are sole traders or very small teams. When I start talking about departments it is easy to dismiss this as something that might happen when you are bigger, but getting your departments sorted out early on is key to a calm and stress-free business.

Let's think about a big business. It will have a sales and marketing team responsible for getting customers through the door. The clients they attract are then served by the operations team, who are responsible for the 'doing' bit of the business, whether that is a product or a service. The third area of the business consists of support services such as Finance, who make sure you get paid, IT, Human Resources, Facilities and Security. All these support services together make up what is often known as a 'back office'.

Each of these three areas are critical to the business succeeding and if you took one out then the business would fail.

In a small business it is very easy to ignore the need for these three departments and to focus on operations or sales and marketing, letting the other areas slide. Acknowledging you need the three departments and taking steps to ensure each department gets time allocated to it will reduce stress and improve cash flow in your business.

Each 'department' has responsibility for different tasks, all of which come together to make the business work.

Client Attraction (Sales and Marketing)	Delivery (Operations)	Behind the scenes (Support Services)
Branding	Products	Accounts
Website	Services	Bookkeeping
Adverts	1 -2 -1	Invoicing
Social media	Groups	Email
Content creation	Online	Management
Speaking	Evergreen	Data protection
Competitions	Nurture	Security
Email marketing	Payment processing	Support systems
		Wellbeing
		Health and Safety
		Recruitment
		Policies

Figure 1: The three 'departments' found in every business with examples of the activities that each is responsible for

Rule 2. There are three stages of business

1. Getting started

2. Going steady

3. Finding freedom

5+ years	Finding Freedom
3 – 5+ years	Going Steady
Up to 3 years	Getting Going

Figure 2: The three stages a small business will typically go through

Getting Started is a longer phase than most people think it will be and lasts for about two years for many business-es, but can be longer. This is the stage when you are finding out exactly what it is you want to do and learning how to speak to your clients in a way they will under-stand.

Going Steady: Once you have some ways of working that are repeatable and you know will bring in some sales, you have reached the Going Steady phase. Con-gratulations! Many people are happy to stay at this lev-el forever, adding a few new things from time to time and tweaking their offer and that's great. Some peo-ple will want to move to the third level, which is Finding Freedom.

Finding Freedom is the stage where you start to extract yourself from the business so that it can run itself. This could mean that you bring staff in to do the work or you use a franchise model to expand your business. The key is that you are doing less and less of the work yourself.

Depending on which level of business you are at, there are systems and tools that will be appropriate for you to use and some which are not.

	Client Attraction	Delivery	Behind the Scenes
Finding Freedom	Sophisticated launch strategies	Employees Franchisees	Increasingly automated Employees or outsourced Clear operating procedures
Going Steady	A repeatable strategy to get new clients Joint ventures Clear marketing plans	Standard approach to delivery Reduced decision making Confident in products and results	More sophisticated technology Simple automations Outsourcing specific tasks
Getting Going	Play with your offers and message Find out what works!	Start getting customers Collect testimonials Respond to feedback Tweak your offers	Testing different systems Creating simple processes Start to use the tech to help you

Figure 3: The core activities for the three business departments at the three different stages of business

If you are in the Getting Going phase then you should be Experimenting. You need to be working with an open mind and be ready to play with the way that you work to find the way that works best for you. Don't feel like you need all the answers, and it's fine to have a few unexpected explosions along the way!

Once you know 'what' and 'how' in the Going Steady phase then you are ready to start Systemising! This will make running the business more straightforward, requiring less mental effort from you and allowing others to start to help you as you reach the dizzy heights of Automation and Delegation, which will eventually lead to the Finding Freedom stage.

Action: Identify your stage of business and think about the activities you are currently doing. Do they fit with the framework?

Before you start choosing your systems and tools

Before you get started using any systems for your business, it is helpful to have an idea of how you want it to look. One of the benefits of running your own business is that you are in charge and you make the rules. It's easy to be constrained by our expectations of how a business runs but try not to be! Companies like Uber (a taxi company with no taxis) and AirBnB (a bed and breakfast company with no properties) are a great example of this. While I am not suggesting you need to develop a completely new business model, it is good to start as you mean to go on. If you only want to work four days a week then start there, and if you want to pick your children up from school every day then set your working hours to finish at 3 pm. Sure, there will be some people who won't buy from you because of this but that's ok. There's usually more than enough business to go around and delivering superb services and products to people who are happy with your business model will make running your business so much more enjoyable.

Things to think about:

- What will your working hours be? Will you work weekends? Occasionally/never?
- How will people contact you?

- Will you have an email address for work? Will you have a separate phone number to your personal number so you can 'switch off' out of hours?

- How will people contact you out of working hours or when you are busy with work? Will a voicemail be enough (and if so do you have a message for your clients; this is easier if you have a work-only phone)? Would it be beneficial to use an answering service so that your clients speak to a real person?

- Do you want/need a physical location for your work or would like to be 'location independent'? If you are working from home, are you happy to share that address with people (there are times where you need to give a physical address legally)? If you are not happy with sharing your home address you can rent an address from your accountants, or a local shared office will often offer this service.

How will you do your work?

The most straightforward scenario is a bricks and mortar business where you know you will need to be present at the site for the times you are open.

If you are selling physical products online, will you be shipping them yourself or will you be using a shipping service? Amazon now offer this as a part of their seller packages so if you don't want to be tied to having to post things out, this can free you up, but at a cost. If you are shipping things yourself, which delivery service will you use? There are many alternatives to Royal Mail now and finding the one that offers the right flexibility and cost for your business is a key part of making your business work for you.

If you are a services business, are you working with clients one-to-one? Is this done in person or are you using a video conference service like Skype or just telephone calls? Do you run workshops or group programmes where you are offering your services one-to-many? Again, these can be either in person or online, with technology now making it easy to run virtual workshops, courses and even conferences.

It may be that you plan to do many of these things, but if you are starting out I would suggest that you stick to just a couple of methods and plan to build in the others later. This allows you to get good systems for the methods you have chosen, to make mistakes and learn from them so that you don't repeat them as you expand.

Action: Decide on your phone number: personal and business combined or separate business number.

Action: Working hours: make sure you are clear about this in your diary and block off your 'non-working' time.

Action: Consider whether an answering service would be a good solution for your business.

What is your business?

As well as thinking about how you want to work, it is also important to be clear about what your business is and who your clients are.

This will help you to build a business that serves those clients well and which will in turn help you to enjoy it more and to be more profitable. For example, if you are offering children's parties, you are unlikely to get many customers from LinkedIn, which is mainly focused on a business environment, and running your business during school hours only is unlikely to make it successful.

As a minimum, you should know your business name, and be able to describe what your business does in one or two sentences. Being able to describe your business quickly is key to being able to spread the word about it. If you can tell everyone who asks in a succinct way so they really understand it, they are more likely to remember you and refer you onto other people.

Another thing that is worthwhile doing is thinking about the personality of your business and describing it in three to five words. Look at the following words and pick the ones that most resonate with you. These will help you when you are creating anything new for your business.

Action: Identify three to five words that you feel represent your business.

Adventurous	Agreeable	Ambitious	Artistic	Bold	Brave
Bright	Calm	Capable	Caring	Casual	Charming
Cheerful	Chic	Classic	Collaborative	Colourful	Confident
Conservative	Contemporary	Convenient	Cool	Curious	Cooperative
Creative	Credible	Cultured	Cutting Edge	Daring	Decisive
Detailed	Determined	Different	Diligent	Discreet	Dynamic
Eccentric	Educational	Efficient	Elegant	Enchanting	Encouraging
Enduring	Energetic	Entertaining	Enthusiastic	Ethereal	Excellent
Exciting	Exuberant	Fabulous	Familiar	Fancy	Fashionable
Formal	Frank	Fresh	Friendly	Fun	Functional
Funny	Futuristic	Generous	Gentle	Glamorous	Happy
Harmonious	Helpful	Hilarious	Hip	Impartial	Impressive

Industrious	Informal	Innovative	Inspiring	Inviting	Jolly
Joyous	Kind	Knowledgeable	Likable	Lively	Lovely
Lucky	Lush	Mature	Mischievous	Modern	Natural
No-nonsense	Nostalgic	Novel	One-of-a-kind	Organic	Playful
Predictable	Productive	Professional	Proud	Quiet	Quirky
Radiant	Rebellious	Receptive	Reflective	Relaxing	Reliable
Responsible	Retro	Revolutionary	Rural	Rustic	Secure
Sensitive	Serious	Simple	Sincere	Sleek	Smart
Soothing	Sophisticated	Steadfast	Stimulating	Stylish	Talented
Tasteful	Thoughtful	Thrifty	Trendsetting	Tough	Trustworthy
Unbiased	Uncomplicated	Unconventional	Unique	Urban	Versatile
Vintage	Warm	Whimsical	Witty	Wise	Youthful

Finally, think about the colours that you might want to use in your business. There are lots of studies that have shown that different colours create different types of feelings or emotions in us, and it is helpful to understand this when we are using colour in our business.

- Blue is a colour of calm, respect and trust, so is often used in corporate branding. It's the world's favourite colour too!

- Red is a colour of excitement and has been shown to reduce rational thinking; some companies even charge more to insure a red car! It's also high energy, so it's great for an events business, but not so suitable for a therapist.

- Green is about nature;

and so on.

If you want to know more about this, then Google 'colour psychology in business'. So much interesting research!

Action: Complete the bonus worksheet 'My Business Branding' available from the book downloads at www.alicejennings. co.uk/book-bonuses

Who are your clients?

As well as thinking through the personality of your business, it is a good idea to think about the personality of your clients. Marketing consultants will often create a client avatar, or ideal client for a business when they are developing marketing strategies for them, and this is a good idea for your systems too.

An ideal client avatar is a fictitious person who would be your perfect client. If you could only ever sell to one person again who would it be? Which customers have delighted you and made you LOVE your business?

Think of the traits that contributed to this and use them to create an individual who you will build your business for. At this point, some of you will be rolling your eyes and saying, 'But I can help anyone!' or 'Everyone needs my socks!', which may be true, but it is much harder to build a relationship with everyone than it is with an individual.

If you don't have an ideal client then take five minutes to work through the Who are your clients? section of the workbook and get a feel for who you are trying to connect with. If possible avoid broad-brush approaches like 'middle-age men' and talk instead about Richard, 52, from Hertfordshire. Give it a try – it really works!

Action: Complete the bonus worksheet 'My Business Ideal Client' available from the book downloads at www.alicejennings.co.uk/book-bonuses

The bigger picture

Defining your business goals and thinking about your ideal customer should not be an isolated exercise you do every January and then forget about till the next year. It should inform everything you do in your business, every day.

This book is not about business goals, but if you haven't set your business goals for the year, quarter and month then I recommend that you do so. As you work through the book and find recommendations that appeal to you, ask yourself how they support the delivery of those goals. Every system that you have in your business should support at least one of your goals. Otherwise they have no place taking up your time and resources.

This may seem harsh but it never fails to surprise me how many people are paying for systems that they never use. Many are just £9 a month so it doesn't feel much but five unnecessary systems at £9 a month is costing you over £500 a year!

Start to get into the habit of asking 'How does this system support my business goals?' and if you can't answer it then don't do it!

Chapter 1 checklist

The checklists are designed to help you decide what you need to do in your business. Not all activites are relevant to all businesses so choose those that are applicable and identify whether the activity is something to do now or in the future.

Action	Not relevant	For the future	To do now	Done it!
Download the worksheets from www.alicejennings.co.uk/book-bonuses				
Identify your stage of business and think about the activities you are currently doing. Do they fit with the framework?				
Decide on your phone number: personal and business combined or separate business number.				
Working hours: make sure you are clear about this in your diary and block off your 'non-working' time.				
Consider whether an answering service would be a good solution for your business.				
Identify three to five words that you feel represent your business.				
Complete the bonus worksheet 'My Business Branding'.				
Complete the bonus worksheet 'My Business Ideal Client'.				

Chapter 2

Client attraction

Getting customers

In the SORTED Framework, the first business department is Client Attraction. Getting customers is key to your business being successful, and getting the balance right between bringing in sales and being able to deliver on the sales is something that is tricky to get right!

While it may seem counterintuitive to start with these systems, if you don't have the 'back office' sorted there is often a delay between starting marketing activities and getting paying clients. While having your back office systems sorted is important, it's not going to bring in the money so get some client attraction systems in place first, then focus on the day-to-day systems.

There are lots of different ways to get customers or clients, and technology has opened up new avenues that make it much easier to compete with big businesses. While this is great for giving you options, the downside is that it can result in doing lots of things badly rather than just a few really well. The way to avoid this trap is to pick one just one or two things to start with and bring in more as you get established.

Word of mouth

This is the simplest and cheapest way to get clients – going out and telling people what you do, and those people telling other people. This can work brilliantly, particularly for a local business or anywhere that recommendations are important to build trust.

While you don't really need a 'system' for basic word of mouth, it is worth thinking about how you might acknowledge people who recommend you. 'Recommend a friend' discounts, where both the recommender and the new customer get a discount or bonus, can be a great way to encourage people to spread the word about what you do. If that's not appropriate, then a simple bunch of flowers or a thank you note to existing customers who are sending you sales can do the trick.

Offline advertising

I'm not going into any detail on this other than to say that for some businesses offline methods work best so don't think you have to be all over social media to have a great business.

Traditional print advertising such as flyers, posters, advertising in newspapers, parish magazines and so on works really well, particularly for local businesses.

Networking also falls into this offline category of client attraction, and local networking groups can be a great source of clients, particularly for business-to-business services.

Speaking at events can raise your profile and bring clients. Speaking opportunities give you the chance to share your message with larger groups of people than you would be able to reach and if you enjoy being on stage can be a great way to get clients.

Just because there are lots of great online ways to connect with customers doesn't mean you have to use them. Experiment with offline as well as online and find the ways that work for you and your customers.

Action: Decide what, if any, offline client attraction methods could work for your business.

Email marketing

What is email marketing?

Email marketing is telling potential (or existing) customers about your products and services by sending them emails. These could be newsletters or special offers but would be sent in bulk to all the people who subscribe to your 'list'.

We all groan inwardly now when someone asks us for our email address. Shops are starting to ask for email now when we pay, offering to send us our receipt by email; everyone is being bombarded by hundreds of emails each day and it can become overwhelming. (If you are one of the overwhelmed, then Chapter 4 has some great tips for you!)

However, despite this rise of email traffic, email marketing is still a very effective way of getting in touch with your clients. Think of your own emails; I bet there are a few marketing emails you open as soon as you see them hit your inbox. These are probably emails that are giving you really great information, services or deals and are consistently delivered, meaning you don't want to miss out.

If you decide to use email marketing then you want to fall into this category. Be sure you know who you are targeting, make sure that your emails are full of great value for your ideal clients, and don't send too many emails (or too few).

To make email marketing easier there are a number of different services you can use which make it easy to send bulk marketing emails, allow people to sign up for your email list, track the effectiveness of the email campaign (this is what a newsletter or marketing shot would be called in the system) and more. The alternative is sending a group email from your normal email. Please don't do this; it risks your online reputation and is not easy to do within the regulations I go on to describe here.

Once you have decided to send emails for marketing purposes, you need a few basics in place:

1.   You need to know the rules.

2.   You need to choose your provider.

The rules of email marketing

It is really important to stick to the rules when you start email marketing. At first the rules can seem quite complicated but they boil down to a few key principles, and as long as you have some basic respect for your potential clients then there should be no problem sticking to them.

The Information Commissioner's Office (ICO) oversees the collection and legal use of personal data in line with the General Data Protection Act (2018). It is essential that you understand your obligations as a business owner to keep any personal data you hold legally (which includes names and email addresses).

You should also check whether you need to register with the Information Commissioner's Office. This is easy to check by taking their quiz at www.ico.org.uk (to be fair, they are trying to make Data Protection fun!)

There are a number of things you need to do to be General Data Protection Regulation (GDPR) compliant. I'm only going to mention here the ones you need in place to use an email marketing tool so please check the resources section for a wider view of the regulations.

In order to use email marketing correctly:

1.   You must be really clear on your reason for using people's email addresses. For most small business owners this means having explicit permission to market to them. You must not add people to your list without telling them. Meeting someone, networking and getting their card does not count, and someone making a purchase from you does not count unless they tick a box to opt in at the checkout. Be clear and upfront with people about what you are going to do with their email address. (They will be much more engaged if they

actually want to hear from you and this is a really good thing!)

2.   You must provide a simple way to unsubscribe; using an email marketing product deals with this for you. The little button at the bottom that says 'unsubscribe here' covers this beautifully.

3.   You must give your address; it is a legal require-ment that you put your address at the bottom of all marketing emails. If you work from home and don't want to do this, then you can pay for a reg-istered office. Many accountants offer this service as do some chambers of commerce and shared offices.

4.   You must not behave in a deceitful manner; you can only do what you say you are going to do. You must not say that you are going to email people about yoga classes and then, when your friend starts a business selling cars, start emailing them about that. That is considered deceitful. (If your friend does start a business, you could email your clients telling them about it and suggest they sign up to his list BUT you cannot automatically move them to the new list without their explicit permission.)

5.   It must be possible for subscribers to get a copy of the personal information you hold about them and also to request deletion from your records.

Single vs double opt in

Single vs double opt in refers to the way that someone signs up to your email list.

Single opt in is where someone enters their email address into a form and they are added straight to the list without any confirmation step.

Double opt in means that when someone signs up for your list, you must send them an email asking them to confirm they want to be on the list and they must click through to confirm, before they are added to the list.

Which is better? One of the things you are required to do under GDPR is show that people definitely signed up for your list. Without the confirmation step it is possible that anyone could enter your email to the list without your permission.

You will always lose people who sign up but never confirm their intention to be on the list, but the people who do get onto the list will be more committed that those using single opt in.

What does an email marketing tool do?

There are three areas that most email marketing tools will cover. They sometimes use slightly different terms but they are generally doing the same thing.

Collect and manage email addresses

Firstly, they enable to you collect email addresses to build your list. A list is a collection of email addresses and usually first names for people who all share the same interest and would like to hear from you on that subject. Under some circumstances you may want to collect more than just the basic name and email, but avoid this unless it gives you a real advantage as people don't like giving away information for no clear reason.

When would be a good time to collect extra information? If you have a specific use for it. Good examples of this might be a photographer specialising in newborns who might ask for a due date so they could send some reminders to book your session in, a party planner who may ask for a birth date so that they can send special offers, or a local business covering a few geographical areas requesting information on the town you are in so they can tailor emails to only send offers applicable to the subscriber.

When you are asking for the extra information, it is always good to explain why you want it. People are much more likely to hand it over if they understand how it will benefit them to share it with you.

So we have our list, with a few different fields (this is the term used for the name, email and any other information, i.e. date of birth).

Getting people onto your list

The next challenge is to get people onto the list. Assuming you are following the rules above, then there are two main ways to get people on the list. Firstly, they can give you their email address on a piece of paper and you can manually add it or they can add themselves using an online form. For manually added addresses, you can typically do this either one at a time by adding the email address and name into a box, or you can import a larger number (anything from one to thousands) from a spreadsheet. Remember you can only import people to your list if they have given permission, so keep any paper-based sign-up forms as evidence of this.

If you import you will need to organise the data into the format that the email management package is looking for, typically with the email address in the first column, the name next and then other data afterwards, and as you import the data you will be asked to map the columns in the spreadsheet to the fields of your list. Sit back and wait and your list will be imported. This is great if you have been out and about and collecting emails at events.

As well as offline email collection, you will want to be able to collect email addresses from your website and possibly your social media accounts. This is all possible with the email marketing tools providing forms to put on the internet to collect the data. You firstly design your form in the email management tool and then you get some gobbledygook looking code which you pop on your website and bingo! A form magically appears. Some providers also offer social media integration which allows you to have a tab on your Facebook page that people can sign up on.

Most providers also provide a URL or link for you to share which has its own web page, so even if you don't have a Facebook page or a website you can still share the link and people can sign up for your list. This is one of the first things you could do in a new business, enabling you to quickly collect details of potential clients and email them with news and offers, helping you to build your client base before you even have a website or other web presence.

Send out group emails (which look personal!)

Now we have some lovely people on our list, the next step is to send them an email. Depending on your system this is typically called a 'campaign' or 'broadcast'.

All the providers offer templates, which are predefined, well-designed layouts which you can choose from or you can create your own using your logo and brand colours.

Creating a blank template which has your logo, contact details, social media links etc. is one of those tasks that takes a little time upfront but which pays dividends down the line. I bet you can remember at least one email you have received where there was something left over from the last time it was sent that the writer forgot to delete. It doesn't look great and it's easy to avoid.

Once you have a blank template which looks great, all you need to turn that into a campaign or broadcast is to add your text.

Automatically send email on your behalf

All the previous steps of email marketing are reactive; you sign people up to a list and periodically send a man-ually created email containing your business news and offers.

Automations, as the name suggests, are a way of emails being sent while you sleep. An automation can include sending a series of emails to a new subscriber to help them get to know you better, sending a 'special offer' email to a subscriber who has added something to their online shopping basket but not completed a sale, or sending an email to someone who hasn't opened your emails for a while encouraging them to re-engage with you.

As your business moves from experimental to systemising, it is worth investing the time in creating automated email sequences that will enable you to show your value to customers without doing any extra manual work.

Which system to use?

Mailchimp

One of the most well-known companies in the email marketing arena is Mailchimp. In fact, they are so popular that people talk about sending a 'mailchimp' when they mean a newsletter. Mailchimp has been around for a while and has a lot of things going for it for small business owners who are trying to keep in touch with their clients, as well as a few things that aren't so good. So let's take a look.

Mailchimp started in 2009 and is used by over 15 million people. It was one of the first companies to take a more humorous angle with their product and there is a little animated monkey that pops up all over the place.

The key thing about Mailchimp is that it has an amazing free version. You can have up to 2,000 subscribers (people on your list) for free and send up to 12,000 emails per month (total email send, not 12,000 each. That would be a bit much!)

Mailchimp is not the most intuitive system to use but can be a great starting point for many businesses.

MailerLite

A good alternative to Mailchimp is MailerLite. It's easier to get started with than Mailchimp and offers more sophisticated tagging and grouping of users, so it's more likely to grow with you.

It also offers a great free plan which comes with email support (Mailchimp doesn't offer support at all on its free plan).

Moving on from free tools

As your marketing becomes more sophisticated you might find you want to do more with your emails than either Mailchimp or Mailerlite are able to deliver. Fortunately there are alternative systems that offer more sophisticated features.

ConvertKit

ConvertKit is a step up from Mailchimp and is designed to make it really easy to collect emails from different places on your website. It is great if you want to be able to offer multiple free things, allowing you to 'tag' people when they download specific things and then trigger automations based on that action.

You can then send emails to just the people on your list who have downloaded the free thing by selecting the tag.

Convertkit also has simple landing pages built in so you can create a lovely-looking sign-up page in seconds or you can drop a form onto your own web page equally quickly.

Active Campaign

Active Campaign offers some very sophisticated features at a very reasonable price. It allows you to add tracking codes to your website enabling you to target people from your email list who visit particular pages on your website. It also has very powerful email automation sequences which allow you to send different emails depending on whether a contact has opened the previous email, or clicked on a link within it.

The basic version is let down slightly by its sign-up forms which are a bit clunky to use but it is excellent value for a business that wants to be able to personalise email marketing to potential clients based on their interest in different emails and website pages.

This means you can do far more with this system than the more basic tools on offer, but don't forget that just because you *can* doesn't mean you *should*! Think about how your customers interact with you and work out if having a fancy email marketing tool like this will really bring you value or whether a simpler system like Mailchimp might be more than adequate.

Keap (used to be Infusionsoft)

Keap is much more than an email marketing tool but needs a mention because it is widely used by smaller businesses, particularly those based largely online. Keap brings together email marketing, payment systems and customer relationship management into one integrated tool. It allows you to build sales funnels which can trigger different actions depending on what the contact does. For example, if they view a particular page of your website they may receive a specific email sequence.

Keap is incredibly powerful but also quite complicated and more expensive than the other options. If it is not set up correctly, it can be difficult to use and so it is always best to get expert advice if you are planning to upgrade to use it.

Action: Decide if email marketing is going to be a key part of your client attraction strategy and set up an account if so.

Websites

Twenty years ago, you would start a business with a business card and some flyers. In some ways, this made things easier, but the digital age has allowed us to reach many more people and target those that are more likely to become our customer.

One of the big changes is the arrival of websites. There was a time not so long ago when you needed to have a website hand-coded; literally line by line. This was definitely a specialist job. Now there are many ways to get a website online and the simplest of these are possible even for the most technophobic of business owners. So let's take a look at the options.

Before we get going I want to make clear that to a certain extent you get what you pay for. A bespoke, hand-crafted and high-end designed website will almost certainly bring more traffic and drive more sales than a self-built one. This does not mean that the self-built one is wrong. It's all a question of getting that balance, and starting with self-built and moving to a more sophisticated site as your business grows is a great solution.

Domain names and web hosting

You need two things for a website to work: a domain and a web server to host the site. It is easy to get confused about what the two do as they are often bundled together.

A domain name. The domain is the address at which your website lives, i.e. www.mywebsite.com

Web hosting. Web hosting provides space on a server that 'hosts' the website, and for which you pay rental. The server space is a large computer that is permanently on so that people can access it 24 hours a day.

Some companies sell just domain registration, some sell just hosting, and some sell both together. There is a view that you should use two separate companies so that if there is a problem with one then you are only in half as much trouble, but as many web hosts also offer a free domain with their hosting then it is not always practical to stick to this.

The domain registrar will hold a record of the name of the server (nameservers) where your website lives (hosting). When someone types in the domain name the registrar will redirect the user to the correct site in a matter of seconds. Records of which server each domain points to are held across the world, and if you make a change to your host then your web developer may talk about the records propagating, which is the changed details being passed across the globe to all the different registers so that everyone knows where the new site is.

What do you want from a website?

When you decide to start building a website, whether you are doing it yourself or paying someone else to do it for you, you need to start by asking what the primary purpose of the website is. When combined with your understanding of the customer you are trying to reach out to (your ideal customer), it will help you to make decisions about how the site should look and function.

Start off by thinking about the overall purpose of the site. The main purpose could be:

- *Brochure*: giving information about your product or services and details of how to get in touch.

- *Expertise*: a website specifically designed to showcase your expertise and help people to understand how you work, why they should work with you rather than anyone else, and help people searching for experts in your field to find you and get in touch.

- *eCommerce*. The fancy word for selling online; this kind of site has an integrated shop which enables customers to order and pay online for goods or services.

Once you have decided the main purpose of your site then it's time to focus on your clients and think about exactly what you are trying to achieve with each page.

Included in the bonus downloads for this chapter is my page checklist which goes something like this:

1.   What is the main purpose of this page?

2.   What is the call to action on this page?

3.   Can I easily see what this page is about without having to scroll down?

4.   Are my contact details available from this page?

You also want to think about the journey that different clients may take through your site. Remembering we are all different, it is important to present the same information in a variety of ways so that those who want brief details can easily access them whilst those who like lots of detail are able to find that too.

Get some post-it notes and write the page name of each page you think you may want onto its own post-it. Now arrange them in a hierarchy of items you want to show on the main menu and sub-menus. Some pages can be shown on multiple menus as people may look for the same thing via several different routes.

Think about what other features you want on your site. You may want to include some of the following:

- *Contact form*. Rather than show your email address on your website you may choose to add a contact form which passes a message to you via email. This prevents spammers from collecting your email address and bombarding your inbox with junk.

- *Email opt-in form*. If you have an email marketing list, then you will want to collect the email addresses of people who visit your site and who want to stay in touch. You may offer a free gift in exchange to incentivise them to part with their email address. Some email opt ins are 'pop ups' which appear over the screen after a few seconds. These can really annoy visitors if used badly so make sure that if you use them they are polite, preferably appearing after the user has had time to read what they came for. Also make sure that they don't get the same pop up every visit by setting the display to every 30 days.

- *Photos of you*. Often with a small business, people are buying you. Some high-quality photos of you will make a website more personal and enable people to connect more quickly.

- *Videos*. You may also want to add videos to your website. These can explain more about your product or service or may be testimonials from happy customers.

- *Testimonials*. Reviews from existing customers are really important to help people see how great your work is.

- *Terms and conditions, privacy policies and terms of use*. If you are collecting people's data you need to tell them how you will use it, if you want to protect your content you need terms and conditions, and if you have comments on your blogs then terms of use should all be available on your site.

- *Cookie acceptance.* The EU law states that you must inform people that you are collecting their data. You will be doing this if you have any kind of reporting on your site.

- *Analytics.* Google Analytics provides a free, in-depth tool to understand where your visitors are coming from. Your website host may also offer monitoring. Making sure you know how many people are visiting your site is really important!

- *Backup function.* Depending on how your website is built there may or may not be an automatic backup function. If not then you need to set something up.

- *Security measures.* Again, this depends on what sort of website you have but a WordPress site benefits from some extra security to reduce the likelihood of hackers getting into it. (Other sites won't allow you to add extra security so you need to make do with what's offered as standard.)

Once you have decided on the basic structure of your website you need to decide how you want to build it. It is easy to get a simple website up in just a few hours at a relatively low cost so don't feel that you need an all-singing all-dancing site from day one. A one-page site with a clear message and contact details is a great start if you are on a limited budget or short timescale.

What is the simplest way to get a website?

There are several companies that offer an 'all in' service where you can buy a domain and webhosting as well as a website builder to help you build your site. They typically offer a range of themes, sometimes with upgrades to premium themes at an increased price. The cheapest versions of these websites are often totally free BUT your website will have an address that includes the name of the company, e.g. www.alice.wix.com and there will be adverts of the company's own choosing on your site.

As a minimum, it is worth paying to get the next level of site which should remove the adverts and allow you to have your own domain, e.g. www.alice.com.

If you use one of a range of predefined templates, you are usually able to change some colours and add your own logo and pictures. This makes it easy and quick to get your site live and starting to attract new clients. The downsides of this option are that the things you can change are limited, the themes will also be used by hundreds if not thousands of other websites so it can be hard to look original, and the company owns the design that you are using. It can also be difficult to get the Search Engine Optimisation (SEO) to work as well as it can on a site that you have more control over.

Some of companies that do this are Wix, Weebly, Wordpress.com (see below) and Squarespace.

Wordpress.com vs Wordpress.org

If you've ever felt a bit confused about WordPress then you are not alone. There are two very different things that are both referred to as WordPress with the only difference being the .com and .org that follows. Wordpress.com is an 'all in one' solution from the commercial arm of WordPress which includes a builder and which you pay WordPress to host on your behalf. It is a very cut-down version of WordPress and not what is usually meant when people talk about a WordPress site. If you are using WordPress.com you will go to the page wordpress.com to log in and edit your site.

A Wordpress.org site is one that is built using a free piece of software. The software is open source, which means that not only can you download the software but you can also see all the code and workings behind it. This is not relevant to most users but it means that developers are able to code all sorts of extra functionality into it. This takes the form of themes (look and feel) and plugins (functions) which make it possible to create pretty much anything you could ever imagine. By choosing from the hundreds of thousands of combinations of themes and plugins you are able to build the perfect site for your needs.

When you use Wordpress.org to build your site you need to purchase your webhosting first and then you install the WordPress software onto the server of your choice. You are in full control of the site at all times and if you fall out with your host you can take your website somewhere else. This is not possible with the website builders where the sites do not migrate.

If you have a very particular requirement for your site, such as a dating site or a new marketplace model, you may want to have a bespoke website built from scratch.

This would require a developer to fully understand your needs and then decide on the best way to code the site for you.

As the site will be built to do exactly what you want (and no more), it is likely to be a leaner and faster site than one built with a theme and plugins on WordPress. It should also do exactly what you need!

As the site will have been coded by hand and every programmer has a different way of writing code it will be harder to get help from anyone else to work on the site. For this reason, it is important to choose an established company, preferably with a team of developers so that going forward you are not reliant on just one person to make changes to the website.

Also, if you do choose a bespoke website, be aware that any changes to your branding such as brand colours or fonts could result in quite pricey changes to the website. For this reason, it is important to be clear about your branding before you start work on a bespoke site.

Action: Decide which type of website would be best for your business and take steps to get it set up.

Measuring

Whatever type of website you have, you need to keep track of how well it is working for you. For the website builders there will be some form of analytics available and if you use WordPress then Google Analytics is the go-to tool to understand your audience.

Regardless of which you are using, make a monthly appointment in your diary to check how many visitors you have had, how many pages they visited on average, how long they stayed on the site and what your bounce rate was (bounce rate is the percentage of people who land on your website and immediately leave, bouncing off. We want a low bounce rate as we hope people stay on our site and find out more about us).

Recording this information monthly will show you how well, or otherwise, your site is performing and will help you to monitor the value of any marketing campaigns you may have which direct traffic to your site.

Action: Download the bonus tracker worksheet from www.alicejennings.co.uk/book-bonuses to monitor your stats over a year.

Google Analytics

If you can, use Google Analytics on your site: it will show you not only the number of people who have visited your site but also where they have come from. This shows the most valuable links you have shared or whether your social media campaigns are working.

It also shows you the countries of the visitors, their gender and age and what platform they are accessing your site from (Windows, iOS, Android (phone) etc.). This can help you to ensure that your website is built in a format that works really well for the way your visitors want to access it.

Landing pages

A landing page (or squeeze or sales) page is a one-page website which only allows the visitor to take one action. They are designed to get people to take positive action, either making a purchase or signing up for a free offer to get them onto an email list (see email marketing).

A well-crafted landing page will result in many more 'conversions' (people taking the desired action to sign up) than a badly designed page. There are some companies that only provide landing pages and do extensive research into which styles, images, colours and combination of text get the best conversions. If you are selling online (typically this applies to services rather than products in a store but it may apply if you are only selling one high-end product) then being able to create a landing page is an advantage.

What are the options?

Use a subdomain of your own website

If you use a WordPress site with the right hosting you can create subdomains which are separate websites and which sit under your main hosting. These would have the name landingpage.mywebsite.com (where landing page is the name of what you are selling and mywebsite is the name of your website). By using a theme that has no menus, it is possible to create a landing page for very little cost.

Use a plugin for your website

For WordPress users there are a number of plugins (additional functionality) which can be used to create a landing page. OptimizePress, Beaver Builder and Thrive Leads are good places to start looking. These plugins allow you to build a landing page on your current website without affecting your existing site.

Use your own site

Some themes (notably Divi from Elegant Themes) will allow you to create a landing page within your website with no extra fuss. This means there is no additional cost, just select 'blank page' and start building!

Landing page providers

There are companies which will create landing pages for you. If your business is largely online, and the difference between 5% and 8% conversion rates translates into a significant financial gain, then a landing page provider may be worth consideration. They are not cheap but their templated pages have proven conversion ability and many allow you to split test (i.e. compare two pages with slight differences such as colour or text at the same time).

Companies to look at for landing pages include Leadpages, Unbounce and Instapage.

Social media

Social media has transformed the way that business is done. It has levelled the playing field, and for the first time a small business can really target its audience and grow rapidly without needing upfront investment. For many businesses, social media is amazing.

But (can you guess what's coming?), not every business needs to be using social media. There are so many platforms out there and the one that is right for you will be dependent on your customers and how they want to engage with you.

Social media is about online communities, bringing groups of people together who once would have only been able to meet if they were geographically close. Now there is no need for this as we can meet and interact with people on the internet.

This provides an amazing opportunity for small business owners as we can now connect globally with people interested in our offers. It can also be a huge time waster for small businesses, as the temptation to spend time engaging with people who never become clients can be great.

Social media must be used as part of a wider marketing strategy, and I recommend checking out some of the experts and books in the resources section to make sure you have the wider picture in place.

This section covers only the basics of what the main platforms do and the ways you can set them up to make using them easier.

Facebook

The basics

Facebook is probably the most well-known social media platform, reporting just over two billion active users in late 2018. Started by Mark Zuckerberg while he was at university, it was designed to enable students to interact with each other easily.

Fast forward a few years and Mark is no longer a geek with some crazy ideas, but one of the richest people in the world and Facebook is a global phenomenon.

Everyone using Facebook must start by creating a personal profile with some basic personal information. You must use your own name for your profile, as it breaches the Facebook terms and conditions if you don't and your account can be closed.

Once you have a personal profile, you can then create pages and groups related to your business. You do not have to have a publicly visible link between the two, so there is no reason for your mum to find out you have a business page unless you choose to link them.

Important: It is really important that you do not use your personal account for business, or you run the risk of the account being closed.

Once you have an account you can become friends with people you know (Facebook will magically find them using the contacts on your phone or computer) by sending them a friend request which they must accept before you are 'friends'. Pages can also be liked, meaning you are more likely to see any posts from that page in your news feed.

Your news feed is the collation of posts from your friends, groups and pages you have liked as well as some adverts which display as 'sponsored posts'. Posts can be text, photos or videos which are then placed in the news feed of your friends (on your personal page) or followers (on your business page). People reading the post can then like and comment on it and share it with their followers or friends. When lots of people share a post it is said to 'go viral'. With so many people on Facebook it is easy to see how a post can quickly make its way around the world, being seen by millions of people in a very short space of time.

Facebook uses a top-secret algorithm to decide what it puts into each person's newsfeed (the information they see when they 'check Facebook'). People who either seek out your page or who are shown it by Facebook can like it which indicates to Facebook that they would be interested in seeing your posts, which then means it may be shown in their newsfeed. Be warned though, it's not unusual for less than 5% of your followers to see each post so you need to work hard to be seen. Facebook does offer paid-for posts where you can pay them to show the post to more than those 5% of followers who would usually see it. This is done either by boosting a post or by using Facebook ads.

Facebook ads offer an amazing way of targeting very specific groups of people as Facebook knows so much about its customers. You can target adverts at people who like your competitors' pages, live near you and who are a certain age or gender.

So, who is Facebook good for? It is typically used by people in their free time, when they are behaving as consumers, so if you are selling to customers rather than other businesses, then Facebook could work really well for you.

Twitter

Twitter is a microblogging site. In a short post you give a live update to the world via your profile. If you hate writing at length this could be the perfect option for you!

As with other platforms, you first create an account and then you post regular messages, or tweets as they are referred to on Twitter. You follow people who you think will be sharing information of interest and other users will follow you for the same reason.

If you like someone's tweet you can mark it as liked or you can retweet it, which shares the tweet with your followers. All the tweets of the people you follow are presented to you in your Twitter feed, which is a big long list of tweets. This means you will see a real mishmash of content, especially if you have a few different interests, e.g. if you are a farm shop you may be following local suppliers, other farm shops, local business groups and some parenting groups. This can make it hard to follow so Twitter uses hashtags to categorise content.

When you create a tweet, you can add a hashtag to show the wider world what the tweet is about. Place the hashtag symbol at the start of the phrase, e.g. #eatlocal. The hashtags provide a way of searching Twitter for similar content and therefore connecting with people with similar interests. Once the tweet has been posted, the #hashtag becomes clickable and doing so will return all other tweets containing the same hashtag.

Take a look at your competitors and see what hashtags they are using to give you an idea of how to use them for your business.

Twitter works brilliantly as a source of customers for some businesses and is rubbish for others. Generally, there is more business-to-business connection via Twitter, but go back to your ideal customer and find out if they are likely to be hanging out on Twitter before you decide about whether to use it.

Twitter lists

If you choose to use Twitter then you can group the people you follow into lists, which helps to divide up the different types of people you follow. All your competitors can go in one list, clients another, useful resources another and personal things another. This makes it much easier to interact quickly with the accounts that will give you the best value.

Instagram

Instagram is the social media platform for sharing gorgeous images. Every post must include a picture and the quality of photographs on Instagram is incredible. If you have a business which can produce gorgeous visual images then Instagram could be a great place to hang out. It's ideal for anyone making things, such as food producers, artists, crafters, garden designers and decorators. It's a bit of a challenge to use if you talk about business systems, but just because you don't make a product doesn't mean you can't get Instagram to work for you!

Instagram also uses hashtags very widely to enable people to find relevant content and to connect groups of people together (see hashtags in the Twitter section).

Instagram is owned by Facebook and offers paid-for promotion of posts and the ability for users to click through and make a purchase. If you enjoy creating eye-catching images then Instagram could be a great place to connect with your ideal customers.

LinkedIn

LinkedIn works in a very similar way to Facebook but with a more corporate focus. It was originally a fairly static site that allowed you to share your CV, enabling employers to find new employees and vice versa. Now it allows you to post status updates and write articles which you can share and which others can like and share too.

LinkedIn is great for business-to-business connections and allows you to InMail (direct message) people you are connected to, as well as *their* connections.

LinkedIn is a great place for business consultants and other professional services businesses to connect with potential clients and collaborators.

Action: Decide which platform your ideal clients are likely to be using. Start using that one platform and build an audience and engagement before trying any more platforms.

Social media scheduling

There are an increasing number of social media scheduling platforms available which allow you to post to
more than one platform at a time and to schedule posts
which are added to the platforms on the date and time
specified. This means that in one session of work you can
create posts to be shared over the coming weeks rather
than having to add the new posts each day.

What are the options?

Buffer

Buffer is a scheduling tool that allows you to connect
three channels using its free account and provides an
easy-to-use basic planning tool. The paid-for version sup-
ports more channels, allows more posts to be scheduled
and the reports are more detailed. It has web extensions
for Chrome, Safari and Edge, allowing you to share a link
from your browser to your social media platforms at the
click of a button.

Hootsuite

Hootsuite does what Buffer does but it also allows you
to view the feeds of your Twitter, Facebook timeline
(not your home feed), LinkedIn and more. This is great
for anyone who is attempting to make sense of Twitter
as it allows you to separate the single and often chaot-
ic feed into different subjects using lists or searches. This
means you are more likely to see the important tweets
that could bring business.

Hootsuite offers more features, which can make it complicated and the user interface is not as intuitive as Buffer. However, the free account does allow you to have three connections (see above) regardless of platform. This means you could have your Facebook page plus two other groups and still be on the free version.

Others to consider: MeetEdgar, Co-schedule, Calendy, SmarterQueue and Social Sprout

Action: Decide if scheduling is going to be useful for you and set it up if so.

Chapter 2 checklist

The checklists are designed to help you decide what you need to do in your business. Not all activities are relevant to all businesses so choose those that are applicable and identify whether the activity is something to do now or in the future.

Action	Not relevant	For the future	To do now	Done it!
Decide what, if any, offline client attraction methods could work for your business.				
Decide if email marketing is going to be a key part of your client attraction strategy and set up an account if so.				

Complete the bonus worksheet 'Website Checklist'.				
Decide which type of website would be best for your business and take steps to get it set up.				
Download the bonus tracker worksheet from www.alicejennings.co.uk/book-bonuses to monitor your stats over a year.				
Decide which platform your ideal clients are likely to be using. Start using that one platform and build an audience and engagement before trying any more platforms.				
Decide if scheduling is going to be useful for you and set it up if so.				

Chapter 3

Delivery

Great customer service

Having picked your strategies from Chapter 2 to get clients, you now need to turn your attention to delivering the products and services you have sold them. You will need to focus on giving them an amazing experience with you so that they keep coming back for more and they tell all their friends (taking a little of the pressure off the 'marketing department' as they do!).

How to consistently deliver above expectations

'Quality is remembered long after price is forgotten' (Gucci).

This quote encapsulates why the quality of delivery of your products and services is so important. I know there are people who have delivered superb service to me who I still use as a benchmark for my own work, and conversely, you tend not only to remember bad service you receive but also tell other people it.

Delivering above expectations will create an army of fans who will do your marketing for you. Think about it: a personal recommendation from someone who is genuinely enthusiastic about the product or service they are recommending is so much more convincing than the best-designed website or Facebook ad.

Delivering above expectations as a one-off is pretty easy, particularly in the early days of a business when you are not running at full capacity. It becomes trickier delivering above expectations several times in a row, and it becomes a huge challenge when you are balancing large numbers of orders or clients, a family, hobbies, friends and a dishwasher that constantly needs emptying.

So, what can we do to make delivering above expectations less 'hit and miss', and more 'business as usual'?

Standardisation: over-delivering's best friend

I know that for many people the words 'system' and 'standardisation' send chills down the spine but, I would argue, that is just because you have been faced with bad systems and standardisation.

Standardising your business should free you up, not constrain you. Not having to think about what to do and when will leave your brain free to focus on the important stuff that it can do really well, rather than what to write in an email when someone has requested a refund.

Let's take a simple scenario: a client enquiry.

Someone is interested in your services and sends you an email. What do you do? Start to write them an email reply. Stop. Wonder if it would be better to call. Stop. Look them up on LinkedIn. Wow, they are really impressive. Return to email and start writing a cheerful, not too excited email to offer a time to talk. Check your diary and find some times that you are free and suggest them in the email. Stop. Delete the times and add 'Please let me know when would be a good time to talk'. Delete. That makes you too far too available. Return to diary and add your available time to the email as suggested times. Proofread email. Send. Lie down in a darkened room.

A response is quick to arrive: a chat would be great but they can't make any of the suggested times. Could you do Thursday? No you can't; you suggest alternatives. And get no reply for a week. Every day you wonder, do I chase this up? You write at least half a dozen draft replies and delete. Lie down in a darkened room. Repeat.

You can carry on like this for weeks. Just thinking through the whole process is exhausting never mind doing it, probably for multiple people over weeks and weeks.

So, what could we be doing differently? If we standardised this enquiry process then what would we want to happen?

1.   An enquiry is received.

2.   A pre-written email ('canned response' or template) is sent that responds to the bulk of the email including sharing a diary-booking link for the enquirer to book a time to suit.

3.   A short personalised paragraph is added to the template if appropriate.

4.   A new task is created to follow up in three days if there is no response.

5.   Carry on with our day. No darkened room required. Phew!

When we are talking about standard processes it is easy to think that this is something only a big business would do, and it is just not necessary for your work. But simple processes are easy to capture and you can use them to make sure that you deliver super great service every time, and to explain to people supporting your business – e.g. VAs (virtual assistants), new employees, collaborators – how your business works.

So how do we define a process? However it makes sense to you and the other people who use it! As with pretty much everything mentioned so far, there is no right or wrong way of doing this. The right way is the one that works best for you and your business.

What are the options?

Checklists

A simple checklist is a perfect way to document a system. This can be a Word document or similar, or you could use one of the tools discussed in Chapter 5 which work brilliantly at keeping a list that you can also repeat.

Write out the list in the simplest terms that you need to; don't overdo it but remember that you need it to be clear enough for someone new to your business to understand. Making the list long just for the sake of it will just annoy you when you use it unless you are someone who loves ticking things off!

Simple diagrams

If you are a more visual person then post-it notes are a great way to start. Write each thing that you need to do on a post-it note and stick them to a big bit of paper (brown paper or lining paper are a cheap way to do this). You can move the boxes around to get the perfect order, adding and removing tasks (post-its) as you go. Once you are happy, add some lines with arrows to show how the boxes connect and you have yourself a 'flow diagram'.

Either you can take a photo of it and use it as the 'map' or you can write it out neatly using some software (see next section).

Video

If you are already doing a very standard process yourself but you want someone else to follow it, and the idea of writing a checklist or drawing a diagram fills you with dread, then this one may be for you! There are lots of tools around that will capture your screen as you work and you can create short videos to show people how to do these important, repeatable tasks. This works well for responding to enquiries, uploading blogs and sending newsletters, so start with something like that and work up to the more complicated tasks.

If you are looking for screen capture software take a look at Loom or Screenflow.

If you want a written description as well as the video, there are companies that will create a written transcript of a video for you. Search for 'video transcription services'. At the time of writing, www.rev.com is leading the way in this area.

If all of this still fills you with dread and horror then there is another way. Find a great admin person (either a real one or a virtual assistant) and get them to watch you doing the task. You explain what you are doing as you go along, and they will write it up for you.

Obviously, you will be paying them to do it but it will mean that the processes are clearly documented and you won't have to do it!

Presenting your process diagrams

If you just want to draw out your diagrams so that they are easy to see, then there are a few tools you can use:

- Microsoft PowerPoint, Slides for Mac or Google Slides work fine for smaller processes. You can create boxes and join them with arrows, even using your brand colours to make it look professional.

- If you are trying to map out more complicated processes then you need something a bit cleverer. Lucidchart and SmartDraw are two great tools that are free to use (up to a certain point) and which allow you to quickly and easily draw professional-looking maps.

These can then be downloaded and used either as standalone documents or inserted into written documents (Word, Pages, etc.) so that you have the start of a user manual for people working in your business.

Standardisation tools

There is nothing wrong with a checklist in Word or a photo of post-its as long as you can read and understand what is meant to happen and when. However, if you want it to look a little more professional and you want it to be easier to replicate then there are some tools that can help you out.

Before you choose your tool, think about whether this is something you will be using purely for yourself or with others too. It's also worth checking the Customer Relationship Management (CRM) section before plunging into checklists. CRM systems can manage client-related processes really well.

Checklist tools

There are lots of 'to-do' products that allow you to create checklists which can be ticked off in a very satisfying way. While they are not strictly designed for managing your processes, if you create a master checklist and then copy it every time you need to work through the list then this can work very well.

What are the options?

Most email packages also have built-in task management tools. Outlook, Gmail and MacMail all allow you to create tasks and set dates by which you need to complete them. This works fine for one-off jobs and is a great way to start standardising your business

Google Keep

This is a beautifully simple note-taking app that has nice colours. If colours help you to enjoy your work then take a look. A simple checklist can be copied every time you want to run the new process.

Trello

Trello is covered in more detail in the Project Management section and is much more than a list management tool, but it can be used just to manage lists. It's simple to use and if you are a visual person then it's worth a look. You can create a template list which you copy every time you need to do the activity, and then use the checklist to ensure that you are doing all the things needed to deliver the process as well as possible. You can use different cards to describe tasks as to do, in progress, for review, complete etc.

For more tricky processes

If you have lots of processes or you have complicated steps with lots of different options then a specific tool for the job may give a better result. There are a few tools on the market, with more appearing all the time, so search for 'process management tools'.

Process Street

This is a great starting point and lets you have five processes for free so that you can get a feel for the software and how it can help you track progress through the processes you are using. It would be fantastic for a big launch into a VIP programme where you want to make sure that every last task and email is perfect for your new clients.

It allows you to set up a list and then you 'run' it so that you have to work your way through the list, making notes at each stage if applicable. If you are sharing the jobs between yourself and a team this can be so valuable as you will be able to see what they have done without having to bother them.

Manifestly

Similar to Process Street, Manifestly allows you to create lists. They also have an app so you can run the lists on mobile devices and a Slack (a messaging service) integration, making it super easy to communicate with the other people carrying out the steps. Manifestly is a paid-for tool but with a generous free trial and great support.

How to get started

There are four types of process in any business: things you can't do, things you can do but don't enjoy, things you can do and enjoy, and things only you can do. The things to start documenting are the first two categories, as these will free you up to do things you do enjoy.

Action: Pick a task that you would like to stop doing. Document the process in whatever way feels best to you. Even if you are not able to outsource it just yet, having the process documented will make it quicker for you to execute, and means you will be ready to hand it over when the time is right.

What to do with all this information

As you start building your resources about how to carry out the various tasks in your business, you will want to think about creating a shareable resource. This will form part of the IP (intellectual property) of your business and is something that becomes more valuable as you grow. It is something that is taken into account when a business is valued, and a business with no operating guide would have a much lower valuation than one with a clear manual. Remember if you buy a McDonald's franchise you are essentially getting a logo and a manual starting at around £200k. This shows how important your operating manual is if you are serious about growth.

You can create this information hub anywhere so that it can be accessed easily by others but in a controlled way. You could use cloud storage or you could create a members-only website where it is necessary to log in to view the information. Either way, the critical point is that the information is easily accessible but secure. OneDrive, Evernote or Google Drive are good places to start creating an operating manual as you can share the information with anyone who is likely to need it, while being able to revoke access as required.

Templates

To help you get started with your process mapping there are some standard templates available from the SORT-ED online resources.

These include templates for:

- client enquiry
- product order
- blog post
- event
- refund
- new client

Action: Choose the standard templates that are applicable to your business and download them from www.alicejen-nings.co.uk/book-bonuses. Amend to fit your own processes.

Customer Relationship Management Tools

Customer Relationship Management (CRM) is the name given to software tools that manage your interactions with your customers. All the big corporations use CRM to enable them to improve their customer service. If you deal with a business that has got it right then your experience will be really slick as they will know when you spoke to them, about what, and what you might be waiting for.

For a small business CRM is not essential, but it can certainly take a lot of the stress out of managing multiple clients as you get bigger and busier. It also helps to provide the standard levels of service that were mentioned in the previous section, which in turn will provide fans of your business who will do your marketing for you.

So what does a CRM tool do?

At its most basic, a CRM system might be a spreadsheet which has a row for each customer and simply records their basic details, any purchases they have made, any actions you have taken (i.e. posted parcel, one-hour coaching session), and when you next plan to get in touch with them. A simple spreadsheet is a great way to start your CRM journey as you are free to add any columns you like rather than being constrained by an off-the-shelf CRM system.

Once you get more than about ten clients on the go at any one time, you may want to think about a more sophisticated system. This will allow you to capture all the information about the clients but will also allow you to do more sophisticated things like:

- generate tasks with due dates
- connect to your calendar so that tasks from the CRM are also shown in your diary
- create a standard series of events that you can trigger for any client so that you are delivering standard service

- connect to your email system so that a client record stores all emails between you against their record

- create 'canned' responses to provide standard answers for rapid email writing

- store notes against the client record (i.e. session notes, copies of documents you have sent, invoices)

- share the account with others so that you can delegate work, see what has been done by whom and what is still outstanding.

In short, it becomes the hub for your day-to-day client management. If you are planning to use, or already use, staff in your business then a CRM system enables everyone to see what is going on without having to speak to each other.

Why use a CRM tool?

From the list of features of a CRM tool you can hopefully see how it could be useful. The greatest benefits of CRM come from knowing that it's all in hand. When properly set up and used, a CRM system can do most of the thinking for you, as well as remembering what needs doing when, and this can be a huge relief to a busy small business owner.

To give you a fuller picture of how this works, let's imagine a scenario for a service-based business with a new client.

When a potential client gets in touch they are added to the system as a potential client. They have booked a free consultation and the integrated booking and CRM systems mean there is a record in the CRM system when you go in to look.

You have defined a series of three welcome emails for people who are having a free consultation session. These explain a little more about your business and offer some free resources they may find useful. You trigger the system to send the three emails over a few days, before the call.

During the consultation, the customer decides to sign up. From the CRM, you can quickly fire off the welcome email pack with the terms and conditions, and create a short note against the client with relevant notes from the consultation. You create a task for the day before you work with the client, to send a personal text, saying how much you are looking forward to the session (this is clearly only appropriate for certain business types!).

Once you have delivered the service, notes you make can be added to the client record in the CRM system. This can be repeated for the duration of your work with them.

Once the work is complete, you trigger a task to send a feedback request a week later, and follow up the week after if nothing has been received.

A month later a task is triggered for a follow up to see how they are getting on and to offer extra support if they need it.

A year later the client gets in touch about some further work, and you are able to open their records and flick through to refresh yourself on how you left the situation. The client feels very special that you have remembered their scenario so clearly and immediately makes a purchase.

And that is where CRM can give you the edge.

As a busy business owner, you may have many 'live' clients at any given time, and putting them all into the same system with reminders to contact them at appropriate points in the future means that they all get the attention they require, but you don't need to keep the tasks in your head.

For a product-based business, your CRM system should be integrated into your sales records so you are able to see the types of products that specific customers are interested in and tailor offers to them. Some systems will capture key dates such as birthdays and send discount offers to help celebrate.

What are the options?

Start with a spreadsheet

If the idea of a CRM system makes you feel a bit wobbly, then start with a simple client spreadsheet. You can download a free template for this from www.alicejennings.co.uk/book-bonuses

This allows you to track prospective, current and past clients in one place, and if you set aside a little time twice a week to work through the actions that are due then you will find that you are able to track your clients with minimal effort.

A spreadsheet lets you do some lovely things like conditional formatting which can make overdue activities turn red so you have visual clues about how well you are keeping on top of things. It is simple to use and free (depending on which one you use).

Like every system though, it won't work unless you actually use it, so commit to keeping it up to date for two months by putting a time slot in your diary a couple of times a week and see if you feel it is bringing you benefit. If it is but you wish it did more, then take a look at a more bespoke system. If it is just a pain to fill in then ditch it. If you only work with a few clients at a time then it may be unnecessary but be aware that if you want to bring in external help then a single point of information will make delegation very much easier.

Capsule CRM

If you are looking for an entry-level system then Capsule CRM is a great place to start. With a great free version, the only investment you need to get going is some time. It integrates with your email and allows you to create simple workflows that can be added to any contact at any time.

Connect it to your email account to import your contacts and then create a 'case' for the people you want to manage through Capsule. You can also connect your calendar so that tasks you create in Capsule are visible in your main calendar and you can plan your week accordingly.

Capsule also integrates directly with Gmail so you can add your emails straight into the system, creating tasks and reminders in a few seconds so nothing slips through the cracks.

HubSpot

HubSpot is a more mature product with more bells and whistles than Capsule and can therefore seem a bit more overwhelming.

The bells and whistles do some great things though, like automatically grabbing the emails you send or receive from contacts in HubSpot and adding them to the record (Capsule needs you to send it the email in order for the record to be attached to the contact). HubSpot is free for the basic functions for unlimited contacts. It is a powerful way to get your customer experience systemised and to consistently deliver a great experience.

Keap

Keap (formerly Infusionsoft) was covered in the section on email marketing as it has functionality to do that, but it also allows you to use it as a CRM system. It is more expensive than using two separate systems but if you have plans to scale quickly it may be worth consideration.

Action: Consider whether a CRM system could help you deliver better customer service. Choose and set one up.

Client communication

The way you communicate with your clients is key to the way they experience your business. Research has shown that a company that deals positively with a problem will have more loyal customers than one that doesn't have any problems in the first place! Much of this is about communication so think carefully about how you choose to communicate.

Technology has expanded the options for how you can interact with your customers, which has in turn made location less and less important in many businesses. If you are a service business then you may no longer need to see your clients in person but instead can use one of the video conferencing options.

What are the options?

Skype

Skype allows you to have telephone conversations and video calls with other computer or smartphone users using the internet to carry the call and pictures rather than the traditional telephone line.

Zoom

Zoom is an online video conferencing tool which offers different versions depending on your needs. It is free for a two-person meeting and free for up to 12 people for a 40-minute meeting. It has an integrated recording function and all meeting attendees can share their video and screens at the touch of a button.

Alternatives: Facebook Messenger, WhatsApp and Viber all also allow video calls but these are less reliable than the options mentioned above, and so give a less professional impression.

Action: Consider whether you will need an online video tool. Create an account if you think it will be useful so you are ready to share details if asked.

Creating content

Consistency is important when you are creating content. Don't say you are going to blog every week and then only do it once every few months as this will not build trust with your clients. Having a system that enables you to share content without having to make a decision about what it will be every day may help you to be consistent.

Sit down and plan a month (or three-month) period. Check the downloads section for the book (www.alice-jennings.co.uk/book-bonuses) for a bonus content planner which can help with this. Add in any big pieces of content you plan to create first, then add in the sharing of that content across the different platforms you have available. Then fill the gaps with smaller pieces of content, recycling old blog posts and sharing useful information from other sources.

Plug all your plans into your calendar so that you can see what you need to do each week. Then add in the planning and development time required for the larger pieces of work. This will make you much more likely to actually create them as the time will be in the diary.

Action: Create a content diary to prevent decision paralysis. Download the bonus content creation template from www.alicejennings.co.uk/book-bonuses

Written content

Written content can be created in a multitude of places; find out what works best for you. If you prefer pen and paper then start there, if you are happy on a word processor that works fine or if you are writing a blog you can just type it straight into your website content management system.

Make sure that you make use of your spell checker (and that it is set to the correct version of English!) and be aware that if you are writing blogs in a word processing tool they will carry formatting into the website that makes the paragraphs go all squiffy. This is infuriating but fortunately easily fixed by pasting the text into a simple text editor like notepad (PC) or TextEdit (Mac) which will strip out the extra formatting.

If you can't afford a copywriter to review content, try using some of the online writing tools which review your content. Hemmingway is a free tool that you can paste your text into to measure 'readability'. While you might think that a computer won't be able to do much, it is surprisingly helpful at improving your work.

Audio content

Creating audio downloads or podcasts is a very popular way of sharing content. You will need to make a
recording of the information and make it available to
download.

Recording software

Creating an audio file to use for content marketing is
pretty straightforward. If you have a mobile phone, you
have almost certainly got a voice recorder built in which
will enable you to capture mp3 files (the format you
need for easy audio download).

If you want to use something a little more sophisticated
then Audacity is an open-source (and free) tool which
can be used for recording on a computer and enables
you to set levels prior to recording as well as editing them
afterwards. As it has a lot of features it can be a bit overwhelming to start with, but don't be daunted by all the
settings; get stuck in and start recording.

Microphones

It may also be useful to invest in a microphone if you
are doing a lot of recordings. For recordings when you
are out and about you need a lapel microphone which
plugs into your phone (great for Facebook Live). There
are lots on the market but the Rode Lavalier consistently
gets recommended.

For recordings at your computer you may want a larger
microphone which stands on the desk. The Blue Yeti and
Yeti Snowball are recommended.

Don't let not having a microphone or fancy software stop you. Lots of people have produced perfectly acceptable content without any fancy equipment! Getting started is more important than getting the fancy kit.

Video content

Video is another area that has exploded with the arrival of faster internet connections.

There are two types of video and they each have different considerations.

Pre-recorded videos are getting easier and easier to create. You can either use your phone, iPad or computer with an inbuilt webcam, add an external webcam (of a higher quality than the inbuilt model) or you can use a dedicated video camera. The dedicated video camera will give the best results but there is much that can be done with the built-in cameras on your other devices.

Things to consider include:

- *Stability of the device.* If you are using a tablet or phone it may be worth investing in a gorilla grip stand to enable you to position the device securely so that you are framed in the best possible way.

- *Light.* Some cheap work lights from the local DIY store will enable you to control the light better than having a window with natural light. If you are planning to film next to a window then make sure the light is not behind you or you will look very dark.

- *Sound*. See the comments about microphones and also think about background noise; if you are outside trying to shelter from the wind, the microphone will pick up the wind noise.

- *Quality of video*. Most cameras with a video function will let you choose the quality of the video. Think about what the video is being used for as a very high-quality video will result in a huge file. If people want to watch online then these videos will load slowly. Given how impatient we have become, people might not wait for them to load.

Live video

Facebook and Instagram now offer the ability to broadcast live. Both platforms alert your followers that you are live via the notifications and then save the video, enabling people visiting your page or profile to watch it later.

This is a great way to connect with people and removes the need to be perfect as you are live, so there is not much you can do about it!

Recording software

If you are creating videos they will need to be edited. You can either outsource this to someone with editing skills or have a go yourself using editing software. Microsoft Windows Movie Maker and Apple's iMovie are great places to start. They let you clip out any bloopers, add intros, credits and even music over the top.

If you want more advanced functions then Camtasia is a good all-round tool. It works for Mac and PC.

Webinars

A webinar is an online presentation where the attendees can see the presenter but not each other. The attendees can typically ask questions via a chat box, and on some systems can be unmuted or even elevated to presenter status so they can be seen and heard.

What are the options?

GoTo Webinar

GoTo Webinar is the daddy of webinar software and comes at a hefty price compared with the other tools mentioned. It also offers, in my experience, the greatest stability and reliability.

Zoom

Zoom was mentioned in the video conferencing section and has a webinar offer which builds on the basic meeting function.

Online programmes and memberships

Online programmes and memberships are growing in popularity, with more and more people realising the value of being able to share their skills without having to be in the same room as their audience.

Setting out clearly what you want to be able to do with an online course or membership will help you to be clear about which systems would and would not work for you. There are four methods of delivery outlined below but this is likely to grow as technology develops.

The key thing with an online programme is not to get too hung up on the 'how' of it! Getting the content right is key for the programme to succeed, and it is likely to be a fairly small group the first time you run it. As long as you provide good content that is easy to access then people will get great value from the course. Not making a huge investment upfront allows you to be flexible and tweak the course to the needs of the attendees. Once you better understand your client group you can move to one of the more advanced models, or you may find that simple works just fine!

What are the ways of delivering an online course or membership programme?

By email

The simplest way of delivering a digital course is using emails. The emails can contain attached documents, worksheets or videos and you could use an automation sequence in an email marketing system like Mailchimp or Active Campaign.

If you use videos you could embed YouTube videos or you could link to a cloud storage shared folder. This is quick and simple to set up with very little financial outlay, allowing you to test whether there is interest in the subject and the best way of delivering it.

On Facebook or LinkedIn

This is another simple way to set up a low-cost course or membership. Facebook closed or secret groups allow you to add people to the group only after payment for a programme, and you can add documents, videos and even have Facebook Live sessions in the group to interact with the participants. Not everyone is on Facebook or wants to be, so make sure that your audience would be happy with this method of delivery before you get started.

LinkedIn also allows you to create groups and share files and would be a more appropriate platform for corporate clients.

On your own website

If you have a WordPress website or some of the higher levels of Wix, Weebly etc. then you can create a members' area on the website using plugins or by purchasing the membership option. This allows you to create and protect content within your website. There are an increasing number of online membership sites from dog training to forensic scientist which offer communities of people with similar interests the chance to learn and share experiences.

On a third-party platform

With the rise in the number of people offering online programmes, there are now tools available which will manage all the technicalities; all you need to do is upload the content and press go!

These companies either charge a percentage of the money you make (which they collect on your behalf) or they charge a monthly fee to host your courses, or it may be a combination of the two.

The great thing about these platforms is that they make it really quick to get a professional-looking course up and out there for the world to purchase. Some of the tools also promote your courses to their users, increasing your exposure and hopefully sales.

Tools to consider include Kajabi, Thinkific, Teachable, Udemy and Skillshare.

Events

Running events is a key part of many businesses and can be made much easier using good systems.

The most obvious are the online marketing and booking systems which can save hours of work for the organisers and allow people to manage their own bookings.

Publicity

Facebook has an event option which enables people to create and share events with their friends and followers. This has the added benefit of reminding people of the event as it gets closer and also showing who they know who will be attending, making it more likely that they will actually turn up. Facebook offers the basic event for free with the option to show it to more people using paid-for adverts.

Booking systems

There are many booking systems on the market but there are two main ways that they work.

What are the options?

A self-managed option on your own website

The cheaper option is a website plugin, typically on WordPress but also on some of the other platforms. This allows people to order tickets if you have a payment facility set up and then takes payments and sends a confirmation email to the purchasers. This requires quite a lot of setting up by the organiser and if there are any problems, you are on your own to try and resolve them.

A third-party option where the management is done for you

The alternative is companies that will manage your bookings for you. They allow you to create a profile, create events and sell tickets on your behalf. The more sophisticated systems also allow you to create a waiting list so if tickets sell out you can offer returns to people you know were interested, email all the attendees, and some will even publicise your event for you via their 'what's on' pages.

Some systems charge a monthly fee plus a percentage on all payments, and other systems just charge a percentage of the event fee (plus any external payment fees such as PayPal).

Tools to consider include Eventbrite, Bookwhen.com and Ticket Tailor.

Action: Decide which types of content will work for your audience and set up the necessary systems (audio, video, webinar, etc.).

Chapter 3 checklist

The checklists are designed to help you decide what you need to do in your business. Not all activities are relevant to all businesses so choose those that are applicable and identify whether the activity is something to do now or in the future.

Action	Not relevant	For the future	To do now	Done it!
Pick a task that you would like to stop doing. Document the process in whatever way feels best to you.				
Choose the standard templates that are applicable to your business and download from them from www.alicejennings.co.uk/book-bonuses. Amend to fit your own processes.				
Consider whether a CRM system could help you deliver better customer service.				
Consider whether you will need an online video tool. Create an account if you think it will be useful so you are ready to share details if asked.				

Create a content diary to prevent decision paralysis. Download the bonus content creation template from www.alicejennings.co.uk/book-bonuses.				
Decide which types of content will work for your audience and set up the necessary systems (audio, video, webinar etc.).				

Chapter 4

Behind the scenes

Make your life easier

Keeping it all above board

Legal stuff is not my area of expertise so this short section is much more about flagging up things you should know about so that you can find out the details from experts.

As a small business owner, you will need to make sure that you are acting within the law and while it is tempting to take a 'head in the sand' approach to some of the scarier sounding stuff, most things are not as a bad as they seem once they have been explained by a sympathetic expert.

I have also found that some of the things that feel pretty scary when you first hear about them are pretty straightforward when you get to understand them a bit better.

Things to think about

Registering your business

Depending on whether you are acting as a sole trader, partnership or limited company, there are different things you need to do to inform HM Revenue and Customs (HRMC) and other bodies about what you are up to. In the UK, the HMRC website (www.hmrc.gov.uk) is a great place to find information on what you must do. Regardless of what sort of business you have, you will have to inform the tax office so that they can let you know when to submit your returns.

Action: Register with HMRC.

Insurance

As you are providing goods or services to people you will need public liability insurance as a minimum. If you hold stock you may also want to have insurance in case it gets damaged or stolen and if you have business premises you will need to insure that too. There are specialist insurance brokers who will be able to build a package that meets your specific requirements so it's worth finding a small business insurance broker.

Action: Obtain necessary insurance cover.

Data protection

Understanding your legal responsibilities with regard to data protection is essential for all business owners. With large (£millions!) fines for breaches of the policy, making time to ensure you are compliant is non-negotiable. The way you manage data is dependent on what the data is, and the Information Commissioner's Office (https://ico.org.uk/) has lots of information which is written in an easy-to-understand way.

Taking good care of the information you hold is at the basis of all the regulations, so treat all the information you hold on others like you would want your data to be treated. Use good passwords, don't share data without permission and be clear with people what you're going to do with that information.

Action: Check whether you are required to register with the Information Commissioner's Office (https://ico.org.uk/).

Finance

At the end of the day, we are all in business to make money. You may not want to make pots and pots of it (or you may and that's fine too) but unless you keep track of your money it will be hard to know how effective your business is. And if you don't make money then you either have a hobby or a charity!

As a small business, there are two key areas that you need to think about with respect to money:

- How you get paid and how you can pay others.

- How you record your financial transactions in a meaningful way.

It is a legal requirement to submit your accounts each year and this needs to show your profit and expenses to enable correct calculation of how much tax you owe. If you are self-employed you must declare that within three months of starting your business (UK) and you will then be expected to file regular tax returns.

Lots of small business owners get in a tizzy over the money side of their business and while there are lots of details that you could get bogged down with, the basics of finance for a small business are pretty straightforward.

You need to know some essential figures such as:

- who has paid you, how much and when (invoices sent and money paid to you)
- what have you purchased in order to run your business (computers, stationery, products, supplies)
- what other costs are there of running your business (mileage, heating and lighting of your office etc.).

You need to be able to show all these figures in a meaningful way to allow your accountant, HMRC (or yourself if you are on the ball) to work out how much tax you owe.

Bookkeeping vs accounting

Bookkeeping is the practice of recording all the business transactions that occur each month in your business in an organised way. This means entering the totals of receipts and invoices into a spreadsheet or finance tool. You can record them against different categories to make accounting easier at the end of the year. It is relatively easy once your categories are set up, and as long as you know what payments should be allocated to each category it does not require a specialist financial skill to complete. It is also something that is easy to outsource so if you are someone who spends the month of January surrounded by scraps of paper, swearing about your end of year self-assessment, get yourself a bookkeeper!

Action: Decide if you are going to manage your bookkeeping yourself or use a bookkeeper.

Accounting

Accounting is the practice of dividing up all the money you spend on costs and receive in income, and working out your profit and loss (how much money you have made or lost) and your cashflow (how much money is expected to come in and out of your business). This requires a good understanding of the tax laws of the country. A good accountant should easily be able to cover the cost of their fees by helping you to reduce your tax liability if you are turning over more than £10,000. They will enable you to offset some of your profit against tax in a way that might not be immediately obvious to a lay person.

Action: Ensure you have registered with the relevant tax authorities and got your login details in a safe place.

The finance information you need to keep track of

Receipts

You need to keep receipts for everything that you plan to log as a business expense. These can be in a shoebox, file or scanned in as a digital image. There are many apps that will store them for you, and some accountancy packages have added functionality to store the image of the receipt against the record of the expense, which is great. There are even tools (Receiptbank, Entryless) that you send a picture to and it will read the receipt and add it as an expense (including the name of the supplier, cost, date etc) directly into your accounts tool. If you hate doing bookkeeping, this could be something to investigate!

Invoices

As with receipts there are many ways of generating invoices. You could use a word processing tool, a spreadsheet, or a proprietary invoicing product (Invoicely). Some accounting tools may allow the sending of invoices directly, in some cases also allowing clients to pay online and automatically adding the payment to your accounts.

Reconciliation

When you send an invoice, you will typically get a payment for that amount. You need to be able to show that you got paid for the work you did or products you sold. This can all become a little trickier if you get paid via a third party such as PayPal or Stripe who take a commission on the payment. Say you invoice a client for £10. The client pays via PayPal who then take a commission and pay you £9.75. You have still earned £10 but you also need to account for the 25p charge from PayPal as a business expense.

Tax return

Depending on the set up of your business you will need to provide a summary of your finances to HMRC a minimum of once a year. You can file your tax return online but you will need a login which must be posted to your business address, so don't leave this till the last minute. Late returns have mandatory fines!

If you don't feel comfortable doing this then an accountant can do it on your behalf. Some accountants will do tax returns even if they don't deal with your finances for the rest of the year.

Action: Decide whether you are going to engage an accountant to do your tax return or do it yourself. Find an accountant if necessary.

Accounting tools

Spreadsheets

If I had to place a bet on which system is used most for accounting it would probably be the spreadsheet. A simple spreadsheet that tracks your incoming and outgoing transactions is a great starting place for any business, and most spreadsheet packages have templates included.

The power of a spreadsheet means that as you grow you can start to categorise your transactions and the spreadsheet can grow with you. If you are going to use Excel, it is worth starting with a template that enables you to capture the basic information, and if you Google 'Excel accounting template', there are plenty out there for you to choose from. Alternatively, your accountant may be able to provide something which would be in a preferred format for them, hence making your interactions easier.

QuickBooks

One of the simplest systems on the market is a tool called QuickBooks Self Employed. This system is very simple to use (almost game-like) for reconciling your incomings and outgoings. (QuickBooks also has more complex versions that are more appropriate as your business grows.)

The simplicity of QuickBooks Self Employed also limits what you can do with it, so this won't work for you if you have a more complicated business structure or require the ability to create new categories. However, if you just want a simple and easy way to track your money then it's a fantastic option.

It also comes with a mobile app that allows you to categorise all your payments on your phone with a simple swipe right for personal and left for business. Just like Tinder but for accounting!

A final but brilliant feature of the app is a built-in mileage tracker. This uses the GPS (global positioning satellites) system in your phone to track all your journeys and allows you to categorise them as personal (swipe right) or business (swipe left, with the option to add details of the purpose of the journey).

At the end of the year this nifty little package also provides all the figures to do your self-assessment return (UK). You simply need to log on and copy and paste the totals across to the HMRC site.

The simple-to-understand graphs and charts show you how much profit you have made that month/year and calculates estimated tax owed on that income. (It doesn't take into account any additional income but it does have a place to enter that, so for simple income such as interest, it will manage this just fine. If you have a part-time job then this one probably isn't for you.)

As a gentle introduction to finance online, QuickBooks Self Employed is a fantastic starting point.

Xero

Xero is a step on from QuickBooks and offers a comprehensive solution for a growing business. It connects to your bank feeds, allows you to generate invoices (and get paid online) and can be configured to meet your business needs. It also integrates with lots of other tools (like CRM, email management, time tracking and cloud storage). You can even use it to run your payroll.

As with many of the tools with more powerful functions, once you have lots of options it can quickly become overwhelming. If you are going to use Xero it is critical to get it set up correctly from the start, and I would always recommend finding an accountant who can not only do this but also show you how to use the features that will save you time and money.

Alternatives: Wave, Kashflow, Sage, FreshBooks, FreeAgent.

Action: Decide how you are going to keep a record of your accounts. Sign up

for your chosen software or set up a
spreadsheet.

Getting paid

One of the key activities required as a small business
owner is getting paid. As with many of the other areas of
business, how we get paid has changed a lot in the last
20 years, and we are no longer forced to choose from
one of the few traditional, physical, banks monopolising
the options in the past.

Bank accounts

If you are a sole trader you may be able to continue
using your personal account (check with your bank) but
a business bank account ensures that you are able to
separate your business and personal finances, making
accounting easier.

Most business bank accounts will charge you to bank
cheques and deposit cash. You may also be charged
for making or accepting payments in foreign currency,
and almost all have a monthly fee (after an initial free
period if you are lucky).

Before you choose which bank to use think about:

- where the nearest branch is
- where you can pay in deposits (some banks let
  you use the post office as well as their branches)
- how much it costs to use each of the different
  facilities

- any ethical considerations you might have about dealing with different banks.

Most banks require you to attend in person, with identification documents, in order to open an account. Some banks then allow you to meet with real people in the branch if you have any questions or requirements. If you think you will need to borrow money, it is important to choose a bank where you can build a good relationship with a real person so ask around your fellow business owners to find out where is good and more importantly, where is not so good.

Once you have a business bank account you can accept transfers into your account by sharing your account number and sort code. This is usually a free service and is the way that many fledgling businesses take payments at the start.

As well as the high street banks there is a growing number of internet-based banks offering business accounts. This is great if you are based largely online but may not be so practical if you need to pay in cash and cheques on a regular basis.

Action: Decide whether you are going to open a business bank account and research the best account for you. Open your account.

Accepting card payments

Some businesses need to take card payments in person, online or over the phone. Even if you start out only accepting bank transfers, you will find some people will want to pay by card and you will need a card machine or Point of Sale (POS) machine. This allows you to enter card details and take payment, generating a receipt on paper or via email. The payment companies take a percentage of the money you are receiving as payment, and some also charge up front for the device.

The payment processor that is best for you will depend on the amounts of money you expect to take, and where the individuals making the payments are located. Overseas cards will incur greater costs, and different companies offer different rates depending on how much money you take each month.

Companies to consider include: Square, IZettle, Sumup and PayPal Here.

Action: Choose a method of taking card payments in person if this is relevant to your business.

PayPal

PayPal is responsible for transforming the way that we send and receive money online, and while it does charge a fee for the privilege, it is worth thinking about where we would be without PayPal before you get too worked up about how much it is.

Prior to PayPal, a small business would need to have a merchant account in order to be able to take payment over the internet. This required you to jump through administrative hoops with the bank manager and provide quite a lot of paperwork.

PayPal came along and with just an email address and a validated bank account (which they validate by placing a small amount of money in your account, which you then confirm the value of by checking your bank statement and confirming the code) you are able to easily receive money from all over the world, essentially making global trade possible.

PayPal has two types of account – personal and business – and anyone using it for business purposes must use the business version. It is also advisable to have a personal account for your personal purchases rather than just having one account as this makes accounting simpler. Receiving business payments incurs a fee of between 1.9 and 3.5% + a fixed transaction fee depending on a number of factors including the volume and value of transactions and the location of the payee.

Action: Make sure you have a separate business and personal PayPal account.

Once you get a business account, PayPal offers you a suite of tools to make running your business with PayPal nice and easy, and there are several ways you can then use PayPal to receive money:

- by sharing the email you use for PayPal with someone

- using PayPal.me
- creating invoices from PayPal
- creating PayPal buttons which you embed on your website.

Stripe

Stripe is a payment processor that can be used by developers to create payment options online or which connects to third-party tools such as WooCommerce (for WordPress) or Xero and allows you to take payments directly. They generally have lower fees than PayPal (around 1.4% + per transaction fee) and they pay funds directly into your bank account five working days after receipt.

Action: Create a Stripe account if you want to be able to take payments via third-party software at a lower fee than PayPal.

Information storage

All businesses will generate information. This could be files, images, emails, reports as well as client information and a million other things that you will accumulate over time.

Much of this will be stored on a computer and, as any computer is fallible, it is critical that the information is backed up.

This can be done with a physical hard drive that you plug in to the computer to copy the files from at regular intervals, using cloud storage (i.e. virtual) or a combination of both.

Physical storage

As technology has advanced, the cost of digital storage has reduced significantly and you should be able to pick up 1TB (a terabyte) of external storage for around £50 at the time of writing. This should cover most small business needs as long as you aren't a graphics or video-based business.

Having a physical copy of your files is a simple way to ensure that if your computer gets infected with a virus or other malicious files, you won't lose all your information overnight. However, if your backup is kept in the same location as the computer it won't help in the event of a fire, flood or theft. If you choose to only use a physical drive for a backup, I recommend that you purchase two and keep one at a location you visit fairly regularly (your mum's, a good friend, etc.) and every time you visit, you backup your PC and take it to the second location and swap it for the other drive. This means that you will only ever lose the data from the period of the last swap, which is better than losing everything!

Action: Decide whether to physically back up your data. Obtain the necessary hard drives and diarise a regular backup.

Cloud storage

What is cloud storage?

The term cloud storage is used frequently now, but for the avoidance of doubt I will start by defining what we are talking about when we say 'cloud storage'.

Cloud storage means keeping your digital information (basically anything you would save to your computer) on a third-party server in a location that is remote to you. This could be up the road or on the other side of the world.

Cloud storage rapidly evolved as our internet connections improved and it became practical to upload our files to the remote server. There are now lots of companies offering cloud storage, many giving you a small amount of space for free to get to use their service, before charging for a larger storage area.

What are the benefits of cloud storage?

Keeping your information on your desktop computer is a risky business. If it exists in just one place then there is a reasonable chance that either the data could become corrupt or the computer could fail at some point and your data would no longer be easily accessible, if at all. The sensible thing is to back up the data on your desktop, but that takes time and a degree of discipline to remember to do it regularly. Even with a backup you stand to lose all the work done since the date of the last backup.

Cloud storage, when set up correctly, creates a mirror image of files and folders on your desktop, tablet and phone (wherever you choose but potentially all of these) and stores this on the 'cloud server'. This means that with appropriate access details you can get to your information from any internet-enabled device, and also that the data is 'backed up' every few minutes when you are online. This reduces the likelihood of losing all your information following a physical failure of your device or corruption of your data.

A further benefit of cloud storage is that the data is likely to be backed up by the storage provider in several different physical locations. If there is a problem with one of their servers, making it impossible to access the data, then they can switch you over to the different server and ensure continuity of service. This is all done without you even realising! This sort of 'disaster recovery' was once possible only for established businesses with large enough budgets to accommodate multiple server locations with the associated staff and expertise. Now it is possible for a small business to ensure access to business-critical data through a wide range of potential issues.

What are the disadvantages of cloud storage?

While data in just one physical location may be at risk of physical disruption, you do have full control over it. Unplug your computer from the internet and you can be pretty sure that no one can hack in and steal that information from you.

Cloud-based storage means that you are entrusting your data to a company that owns the servers that the data is stored on. While there are some clear positives of this, if the storage servers are 'hacked' into – a form of digital burglary – then your data is at risk.

Even with all the security measures that the storage companies put in place, it is still possible for hackers to get into the servers and some people don't like the idea that their information is 'out there'.

What are the options?

Dropbox

Dropbox was one of the first companies to make cloud sharing really easy. It has an easy-to-use interface which allows you to share files with anyone with an email address at the click of a button. Dropbox gives you 2GB free storage before you need to start paying for a monthly plan.

Google Drive

Google is very generous with its free storage and gives anyone with a Google account 15GB of storage space on Google Drive, though this does include your email if you use Gmail.

As with the other storage providers it allows you to share a link to an individual file or to a whole folder, making collaboration easy and fast.

iCloud

Apple uses a cloud storage system called iCloud which gives around 5GB of free data to anyone with an Apple device. This will be used to store photos, documents and

to back up the devices. You can also share files and create groups with colleagues and family to enable you to
easily share folders and photo albums.

OneDrive

Microsoft's offer is OneDrive which comes with 5GB of
free space for anyone with a basic account. If you use
Office 365 then you get 1TB of space included.

Alternatives: Box, iDrive, SugarSync

Action: Decide whether to use cloud storage
                     and which provider. Set up and ensure
                     all your business-critical data is backed
                     up to the cloud.

The internet and computers

In this digital era, we can't escape the use of computers.
There are a few businesses out there that run entirely on
paper and if they are happy that way then that's fine.
But if you *are* one of those businesses, and you'd like a
little more time off, then maybe it's time to make some
changes.

Making sure your computer is performing at its best is an
important task to help your business run smoothly.

Basic hygiene

Whatever computer you have, you need to take care of
it. I see people complaining that technology is rubbish,
never works and drives them mad when they haven't

been looking after their computer and so it can't do the job for them properly.

What should you be doing to keep things ticketyboo?

Antivirus

It is pretty much essential to install some kind of antivirus software. This is more important on a PC than a Mac as PCs by their more open nature are more prone to attack, but both require at least a basic antivirus product.

Malware scanner

For extra protection, running a regular malware scan can detect issues before they become a problem. There are some free options out there including MalwareBytes.

Action: Check you have antivirus installed and install if not.

Action: Consider using a malware scanner to increase your security.

Switch it off

What's the first thing that any tech person suggests when something isn't working? Switch it off and switch it on again. While this may seem like some kind of mystery fix for things, it actually allows the machine to stop any processes that are running in the background and start up properly. Quite a lot of the time this works a treat.

Given the instant demands we place on our tech, it is often the case that instead of switching off we just put the device into sleep mode. This means that any dubious background processes that are draining the poor computer's energy are still trundling away in the background. It does mean that your computer is ready to work in a few seconds less but it is not as well rested. Think of it like sleeping on the sofa with the telly on vs sleeping in your bed with a blackout blind and silence.

One simple tip is to switch your computer off completely at the end of every day. This is also a great tip for business owners as well as their computers; when it is all going wrong switch it off, rest and switch it on again later!

Action: Commit to switch off your computer/ phone/other device daily.

Update it

Keeping your computer updated is also essential for keeping it safe. All computer software has 'vulnerabilities'. This is where the code that is used to write the computers allows hackers to break in. As soon as the people who develop the software find out about a vulnerability they start working on how to protect it (sometimes this is called patching) and they will release a new version of the software which fixes that weakness. If you don't upgrade, then you are very vulnerable, because the hackers will know about the weakness. So, update regularly. (Windows updates when you switch your computer off so this is another reason to make sure that you are regularly switching it off and on again.)

Rebuild from time to time

Switching off, updating and using decent antivirus software are all good steps for computer health, but after a few years you can't beat a rebuild. Every update you do leaves traces of the previous versions and even if you delete files that you no longer need, there are still bits and bobs left behind. Lots of people buy a new computer at this point but it is not always necessary. Most local computer shops will offer to service your computer for between £50 and £80. They back up all your data onto an external hard drive, wipe the computer and then reinstall the operating system (OS). Then they put the software back on (but just the latest version, not the 35 versions that were there before!) and add all your data back to give you a sparkly computer. Not as good as a brand new one maybe, but a lot cheaper and worth a try if your machine is less than four years old.

Action: Book a service if your computer is more than a couple of years old and running slowly.

Internet

Being able to connect to computers all around the world via the internet has transformed how we do business. We can sell globally, work with clients all around the world and compete with much larger businesses in a way that was not possible 20 years ago. If you have good broadband then life is good but if not, it can be an immense source of frustration.

What is an internet connection?

When we first started being able to connect to the internet we used dial-up. Do you remember the mweeeeeep, mweeeep, l,l,l, eeeeeeekkkkk,eeeekk noise that your computer made when it connected? Dial-up uses the existing phone line to send information down the cables in tiny little bits. This was great to start with because most of the computers you were connecting to were quite basic, and we mainly sent each other text, which is tiny.

As things moved on, we wanted to send pictures and videos and we wanted our websites to look colourful and have moving parts. We wanted to be able to pay for things online and all this meant that we needed to send and receive much more information down our phone lines. So, the internet connections improved to take this into account; we moved to DSL (digital subscriber line) which was much faster and didn't make the funny noises. This is still what many people are using.

In response to consumer demand, fibre broadband was developed which used optic fibre cables rather than copper, which is what most phone lines are composed of. The information can pass down optic fibre far faster than copper (think motorway rather than B road!) and we can send much more information to each other in a short space of time. It's now so fast that we can even watch videos live (streaming) over an internet connection.

What are your options?

Regular broadband is available pretty much everywhere in the UK with a phone line. Gone are the days of dial-up, and we are using a DSL as a minimum.

If you are lucky you will also be able to access 'faster broadband'. In the UK, the government programme to roll out 'faster broadband' has reached 95% of households. If you don't yet have access (predominantly rural areas) then there are funding options available to help you get connected. You can find out more at https://gosuperfastchecker.culture.gov.uk/

If you live in an urban area then you are likely to be able to get fibre right to the door. This means your connection to the internet will be superfast! Lucky you. If you are more rural, it is likely that the cabinet you connect to will connect to the big wide world via fibre but you may still need to use copper to connect to the cabinet. This is like taking the motorway for most of your journey but still doing the last bit on some country lanes; you get there faster but not as fast as if you had a motorway door to door.

Basic broadband speeds vary, with a standard package starting at around 10 megabytes per second download speed (Mbps) which is sufficient for light use, faster broadband packages typically offering around 38Mbps and the super-fast packages as high as 76Mbps. Test your speed with an online speed check such as the one found at www.broadband.co.uk/broadband-speed-test/

Wi-fi and routers

Wi-fi describes the ability to connect to the internet without wires. This is another genius development and most internet providers will offer this as standard. Your router (the box that plugs into the wall) has a password and any wi-fi-ready device can connect if it knows the password.

If your connection is not great you may also want to plug your device directly into the router. The connection will be better with a wire compared with wireless so if you have an important Skype call or you are running a webinar where you want a strong connection, then plugging your computer directly into the router can really help.

If you live in a very rural area you may never get fibre broadband. Do not despair; there are other options. Satellite broadband, radio technology and even mobile networks can all offer alternatives to traditional broadband.

Action: Check the speed of your connection. If it's slow, check with your provider whether you could get a faster connection and the costs involved.

Browsers

Once you have access to the internet there are a few different ways that you can access it. It's worth knowing a little bit about these because some things work much better one way than another.

The software that you use to access the internet is known as a browser, and it lets you browse through the pages of the internet. The first browser was invented by the man who invented the internet and it was imaginatively called World Wide Web. Others followed and some of you may remember Netscape (offspring of which is now Firefox) as well as Microsoft's Internet Explorer.

While this is all very interesting geek history, you may be wondering what it has to do with you. While there is an agreed way of browsers interpreting and displaying the code that makes up all the websites that we visit, each browser does it in a slightly different way. This makes building websites a bit of a nightmare (useful to know) and also means that some things work better in one browser than another (also useful to know).

What are my options?

Internet Explorer

Probably the most well known, Internet Explorer was part of the Microsoft Windows bundle for many years and was the default for PC users. It has recently been super-seded by Microsoft Edge which you get with Windows 8 onwards. Internet Explorer is no longer supported by Microsoft but is still used by millions of people.

Microsoft Edge

The younger brother to Internet Explorer, this is the new version that ships with Windows 10. It is perfectly func-tional but feels a lot more commercial than the other browsers mentioned, with lots of ads. It does have some extensions but nowhere near the number that you will find in Chrome.

Google Chrome

Chrome is owned by Google, which means that some people love it and some people hate it. It doesn't tend to come as a default so you have to go and download it yourself (for free) from www.google.com/chrome/. In order to get the best from it you also need a Google account (which is also free). The account means that you can save your bookmarks, browsing history and account information and access them from any other computer or smartphone that has Chrome installed.

Google is obviously known for its phenomenal search facilities, and users of Chrome can type their search directly into the browser rather than having to go to Google.com and then enter what they are looking for. This alone may make it worth installing.

One of the great things about it from a user perspective is that Google actively encourage developers (geeks who write computer programs) to create apps and extensions which enhance the basic offer.

Mozilla Firefox

Firefox is a descendant of Netscape, which provided many people with their first trips around the World Wide Web! The company behind Firefox is called Mozilla and they have a very different ethos to Google, Apple and Microsoft. Mozilla is a not-for-profit organisation that believes that the internet should be free, open and accessible to all.

They disagree with their competitors using the data they collect to target us with advertising or to profit from selling the data. If you have concerns about how much information Google is collecting about you then Firefox could be a good alternative.

Why does it matter?

With more and more companies offering software as a service, the way you access the internet is important. Software as a service (or SAAS) is a new way of allowing people to use software. In the 'olden days' we would purchase software outright. You would go to PC World and buy a CD (or floppy disk!) with the software on and go home and install it on your computer. You would own that version completely and could use it for as long as you wanted.

This works well for software that isn't updated and when there is a limited internet connection to enable you to download software over the internet. Now we have much faster internet connections and can download software quickly as well as accessing websites at much faster rates.

This means that we have a new way of using software, essentially leasing it from the provider who then runs it on their servers and allows you to connect and do your work online. You never have to worry about having the latest version as there is only one version available, the latest one. You don't have to install things on your computer and you don't have to leave your chair to get access to all the latest software. Software that you can access like this includes email marketing tools, design tools, scheduling tools and website builders.

Hybrid versions of this model are also available, such as Office 365 where you can work completely online but also can download the programs to your computer in order to be able to work offline. This gives you the best of both worlds as the tools you are using are always up to date but you are not restricted by the need to be connected all the time.

Many of the software programs that you can use through an internet browser are optimised for specific browsers and they won't work as well on the others. It is worth finding out if a particular browser is recommended or preferred before you spend too long banging your head against the wall trying to work out why a feature is not working properly.

Extensions

Extensions are little bits of extra software that you can use to plug in to your main browser to make it do extra things. For me these transform the basic browser into a bespoke setup that allows me to do almost everything from a single screen.

The flip side with allowing other people to provide you with extra software is that you lose control, and so extensions can come with viruses, malware and other nasties. Reasonable care needs to be taken when choosing what to use, but with care they can transform your experience. Check the reviews and always do a quick search for an extension you plan to install to check that it is not a known nasty!

Extensions are covered elsewhere in more detail but examples of what they can do include storing and entering all your passwords for you, capturing web pages as notes, creating to-do lists, writing tweets and much, much more!

Some of my favourites include (in a list that is by no means exhaustive!):

- *Evernote* web clipper, which lets you create a note out of any web page you are on, tag it and add it to a specific notebook while simultaneously stripping out all the adverts and other unnecessary stuff!

- *LastPass,* which stores your passwords for different accounts and automatically populates the login fields for sites it knows.

- *Buffer* and *Hootsuite,* which allow you to create social media posts with a click in their relevant programs.

Email

What sort of email do you want?

One of the first things you will probably think about when you start a new business, after the business name and getting a phone number is 'What email shall I use?'

Choice of email address – webmail or domain-based

Firstly you need to decide what you would like your email address to be. There are lots of free email providers like Gmail, Yahoo, BT etc. and they are very happy for you to use their email address to do their advertising for them by using their domain as the second part of your email i.e. alice@gmail.com or fabface@yahoo.com. (The domain here is Gmail or Yahoo.) This is known as free webmail. Of all the providers, Gmail is my favourite and Yahoo probably my least favourite, as it seems to be the least secure.

While webmail is OK for starting out, I would always recommend that people purchase a domain if possible. The domain is the second part of the email and would also enable you to use the website of the same name, so my domain is alicejennings.co.uk and my email is alice@alicejennings.co.uk.

Action: If the .com is available for your domain then it is a good idea to purchase it. Some people will always type .com when they are looking for a site.

If you are serious about your business, then the £20 investment to get yourself a domain-based email is a great investment.

Where to get a domain

There are lots of domain registrars. These are companies that charge between £5 and £10 a year for a .co.uk domain to register the domain for you. Typically a .com is a little more expensive. If you are planning on building a website too then often you will get the domain registration for free if you buy web hosting from them. The big players in domain registration are 123 reg, Go Daddy and 1and1, but watch out for their cheap introductory deals which quickly become much more expensive.

The domain registrar is responsible for making sure that anyone who types in your domain (either as part of an email or a website) gets sent to the correct place. They keep a note of the server that your website and email are sitting on so they can redirect the visitor or emailer there. All in the blink of an eye.

Action: Decide on a domain name and purchase.

Email hosting

As well as paying for the domain you will also need to pay for email hosting (though again if you are buying website hosting this is typically included in the price). Email hosting means that you are renting a small space on a server somewhere which is (hopefully) always on and which is where your emails will be delivered.

Some domain registrars will offer this service, as do web hosts, and email is often included in a web hosting package, so you may not have to pay extra if you are also planning to have a website.

Google will also host your domain-based email for a very reasonable monthly fee. This allows you to use the Gmail client (client is the name of the software you use to access your email) but use your own email rather than one that ends with gmail.com.

If you are a dedicated Outlook user and would like to continue with this, then it is best to pay for an Exchange account. Your email will be held on a server which you can connect to from your computer, tablet or phone. This will also let you to synchronise your calendar and contacts.

Email client

So now your email is being correctly addressed by the registrar and sent to the hosting server, you need to access that server and collect your email. You can do that using an online tool like Roundcube or SquirrelMail or you can set up Outlook, MacMail, Thunderbird or Gmail to collect that email on your behalf and show it in a pretty and lovely format. You can also connect your email app on your phone if you want so you can get them from wherever you are.

What are the options?

Outlook

Outlook is the daddy of email clients, one that many people are familiar with. It is easy to use with some great features; you can keep your emails neatly in folders, set up rules for different emails and create time-saving, templates.

As mentioned in the previous section, Outlook works best with an Exchange account which allows you to synchronise not just your email but also your calendar and contacts across all your devices. If you use Outlook in isolation, be aware that the email will synchronise but not the calendar or contacts.

Outlook comes included with the Office 365 bundle or can be purchased separately.

With some great free options though, it's really not necessary to buy an email client at all.

Gmail

Gmail is the email client that comes free with a Gmail account. It is designed to be used online though there is an app for phones and tablets which allows you to see selected emails offline. There is also a Chrome extension which allows you to use Gmail offline.

Gmail doesn't work like a traditional email client so it can take a bit of getting used to, but many people find it much easier to use than traditional email. Gmail has great spam filters and also automatically sorts your email into four folders: Inbox, Updates, Promotions and Social so it is easy to see the important things.

It also differs from the other options in the way it stores emails. Rather than physically store them in folders it uses tags to create virtual folders. This means that the email can exist in more than one folder at a time which can be useful for collaborations, or clients that you are working with on a variety of projects.

You are also able to check other email accounts using your Gmail account, which means that you can use it for your domain-based email with a little extra setup. There are also some great extensions for Gmail which allow you to do more than just the basics. These include being able to save emails directly into note apps like Evernote, snoozing emails so they disappear from your inbox until a specified date and time, and creating a to-do list from emails. All clever stuff.

MacMail

MacMail is available to all Apple product users and allows you to connect all your devices and sync your email, calendar and contacts. You will get an email address from Apple, typically a @me.com address, and you can also add your domain-based email to the account.

Mozilla Thunderbird

Mozilla Thunderbird is open-source software. It is free to download and use and works very similarly to Outlook. It is great for email but not so easy to synchronise your contacts and calendar. However, it has the greatest respect for your privacy, not using any of your data for research and the functionality is great. A really good alternative to Outlook if you don't want the outlay.

Email signature

Adding a signature to your email is a quick and simple way to make your emails look more professional, do a little bit of marketing for you and help your potential clients to get in touch.

At the bottom of an email, if there is a phone number which makes taking the conversation to the next level simple, a link to your website so people can find out more about you, and possibly your logo or even a link to your latest blog, then you are demonstrating value for your email reader.

One client I work with even adds useful snippets of news to their email signature (obviously this needs regular updating but it's a great way to be really useful and show your expertise all in one go).

All the main email packages covered here have the ability to add a signature from the settings of the email client.

If you want to take your signature to a new level then you could consider using a third-party tool to add an extra bit of pizazz to your emails. Wisestamp allows you to go even further with your signature by easily including your latest social media posts, blog post teasers, links to surveys; pretty much anything you might want to be included in your email can be added to your email signature with Wisestamp. There is a free version which is a great place to start and if you find that it helps to get your message out there then the paid-for version is worth a look.

The great thing about using a third-party tool like Wisestamp is that it will give the same signature regardless of whether you are sending email from the app on your phone, your email client on your PC or on a borrowed tablet. Consistency of branding across all the platforms will help to make sure your message is clear, and you always look professional and are always giving adding value to your clients.

Action: Set up email at your domain, connect to your preferred email client and add a signature.

Managing your inbox

Getting control of inboxes is one of the things I frequently get asked about and something that can cause a huge amount of stress for a small business owner. If you have an out-of-control inbox then rest assured you are not alone and it doesn't have to be that way!

But why are inboxes so troublesome?

It stems from two things: the huge volume of emails that we get now that every Tom, Dick and Harry is sending us their latest newsletter and the fact that many people use their inbox as a to-do list.

If you only ever have a few things to do, then using an inbox as a to-do list is fine but once you start keeping emails that you are waiting for someone to reply to as well as emails that might be useful one day, it is easy to end up with hundreds of emails and then it is hard to find the thing you need. When you can't find things, you tend to start to get stressed and then even opening your email can become an unpleasant task.

To deal with this, I have created a five-step system which I use to manage my inbox. It is a blend of simple steps and some clever tools that do some of the hard work for you.

Action: Work through the steps and create your own system to manage your inbox with ease.

Step 1: Control what is coming in: unsubscribe to any emails that don't bring you value

The first step to a clear inbox is to control what's coming in. We need to take back control of our inbox and stop seeing it as a place that anyone can invade, but rather a place where we invite those who are going to provide information of value to us to come and hang out.

Firstly, you need to commit to unsubscribe. Instead of deleting emails without reading, open them and unsubscribe. I'm not talking about getting rid of everything; I know that there is stuff you want to read later, and we will deal with this in the next step. I'm talking about the junk that you just don't need and that you are quickly deleting (or just ignoring) rather than taking the extra eight seconds that it take to unsubscribe – I timed it and yes, I am a nerd and proud!

Whenever an email lands in your inbox ask the question 'will this give me value?' If the answer is no then unsubscribe straight away.

Step 2: Create rules

Next you need to set up some rules to allow automatic filtering (or sorting) to happen without doing a thing. All the email clients will do this just in slightly different ways, but they do the same thing. They move emails into folders for you while you sleep. A bit like an inbox fairy that just pops in and does tidying for you.

Rules like this work brilliantly for the emails that you do want to receive but which you don't want in your inbox to distract you from why you are there, such as great information but not time critical.

The way these rules work means you need to tell your computer exactly what will happen at a specific time. Create a folder in your email software called 'Read it later' or 'To read', something that makes sense to you.

Next, set up the rules so that emails from people who send great but non-urgent content is moved immediately to your 'Read it later' folder. Finally, schedule a couple of 15-minute slots into your week to go and read through these emails. Now the emails won't distract you when you are trying to get on with other things and they will all be neatly together, ready for you to read for inspiration when you need it.

Step 3: Create your basic folders

Folders are key to keeping your inbox empty but it is easy to get over complicated. Every time you move an email to a folder you are using up a decision and the more decisions you make the more tired you get. Having loads of folders makes it slow to move emails because you can't bulk them up and you need to find each folder, often among hundreds. My recommendation is that you start with six top-level folders which are:

- Admin
- Clients
- Personal
- People

- Resources
- Read it later (which you created in step 2).

Some of you will be saying 'No! I need more folders than that!!'

And I would say to you 'Why?' The search functions in all the mail clients are brilliant so really, we don't need folders at all. Folders are a hangover from the time when we had actual paper folders and using neat filing was the only way we had to find what we needed. Now we can just start typing a name or date or title and 'pop', the emails are all there for you.

Step 4: Create a to-do folder

There will be emails that come into your inbox that re-quire action. The manual way of dealing with them is to create a folder called Action and another called Wait-ing. Instead of your inbox being a to-do list, all emails that require you to take action can be moved to the Action folder.

This way when you have time to action them you know exactly where to look. Things that you have actioned but which require chasing if you don't get a response are moved to Waiting. At an appropriate time each day you can review the folder and follow up as required.

If you have lots of things like this, then you could even consider a sub-folder for each day so you only look for the actions for that day. Think about how it could work for you and the level of emails that you receive.

Step 5: Clean up your inbox

The final step, clearing the inbox. You should be able to see that before we have even started clearing we have developed a system to ensure that new emails coming in can be dealt with quickly. Now it is time to tidy!

There are a few ways of looking at this as shown in the following three options:

Option 1

Move the whole lot into an Archive folder. Yes, you heard right. Life is short; I'm guessing that your answer to the question 'Do I really need to sort out the entire backlog of my emails given that the search works pretty well?' is NO. Select all and move to the Archive folder (which you have created especially for this purpose; you could call it 'Old inbox'). Bingo! You have achieved Inbox Zero. Which is not so amazing on its own, but what is amazing is that you should now be able to stay there. You have a simple folder system, you are using the automatic steps to move the information emails to a folder out of the way and you might be using a tool to help keep your inbox clear of things that you can't work on just yet.

Option 2

Work your way through the whole inbox and sort it out. Follow these steps to make it faster:

- Search for and select all the emails from clients by email address. Move them to the client folder.

- Search for and select receipts by looking for Pay-Pal, your accountant, any ongoing hosting fees, etc. and move these to Admin.

- Select all the emails that contain free downloads or useful content that you may wish to refer back to and move these to Resources.

- Sort by sender and move all the emails from 'people' like friends, business contacts and other non-clients to the 'People' folder.

- You should be left with emails that require you to take action. If you haven't actioned them and they are a few months old then ask whether you ever will, and consider moving to a folder or deleting if appropriate. If they do need action but you can't do it now, then use the snooze function in Gmail or an Action folder (see step 4) to move them out of your inbox until a time you are able to action them.

Option 3

Both the above options have some issues. There is a third way which is my favourite. Select and archive everything that is more than two months old (or whatever timescale feels good to you). Move it all to an 'Old inbox' folder. Then use the sorting method in Option 2 to sort through all the things you have received within the last two months. This has the benefit of getting you into the sorting habit so that going forward your inbox will stay cleared.

And that's it! Keep unsubscribing from things that don't bring value, move things to folders whenever you can and use those amazing apps to keep your inbox clear of things you can't action and I'm sure you will soon be a master of Inbox Zero.

In the next section, we are going to look at calendars. Making time in your calendar to keep on top of your inbox as a daily or weekly activity will stop it from becoming an overwhelming task.

Once you have the system that makes it easy to clear out, then the job of tackling the inbox becomes much easier.

Action: Create an inbox management system that works for you. Commit to keeping your inbox clear.

Calendars

Time is the one thing that we all have the same amount of; at least on a daily basis. So how is it that some people rattle off more in a day than others do in a week?

There are many books whose sole purpose is to share the secret to time management, schedules, motivational techniques, tips and tricks all designed to get you to achieve more in a day. The first thing to note about all these guides is that *there is no right answer*. I absolutely believe that there is no secret method that will work for everyone and you must find the way that works for you.

At the basis of most time management techniques is the premise that you know what you are up to each day.

This is a critical thing for most business owners, ensuring that we don't get double booked or forget to turn up for important appointments. Some people prefer to use a paper diary and while I love the tactile feel of a piece of paper in my hand, you do need to have the diary with you when you are trying to make plans and this is where they can sometimes let you down.

An online calendar can be accessed from a smartphone, tablet, computer, and can also be shared with other people. My husband and I both work from home and he has access to my calendar. This means he can see when I have early morning meetings booked in and juggle his work to make sure he can pick up the children if necessary (don't tell his boss!).

You can also create multiple calendars for different areas of your life: a birthday calendar, a school term-time calendar, a days of the year calendar (for national teacher appreciation day, pie week, etc. to help with the social media!) and you can switch these on and off to get a clearer view of what's going on.

You are also able to create recurring appointments, saving you from having to re-enter things many times. My favourite networking group is on the Thursday of the month, and the clever online calendar works this out for me, meaning I always know when the meetings are going to be.

Calendar options

As with all these things there are a few options worth considering and it will depend on which email client you are using as many are tied to your email.

Before choosing it is worth thinking about

1. what devices you are going to be accessing the calendar on

2. who you want to be able to view the calendar

3. whether you want them to be able to edit your calendar.

Outlook calendar

If you are a Microsoft Outlook user then it is tempting to use the calendar that comes with it to manage your diary. This is probably one of the most widespread calendars and is used within many businesses, so it is familiar to those business owners who have worked in a more corporate environment. What's wrong with it?

You must have an Exchange account for it to sync across all your devices. As this is the main value of an online calendar, then without this it is fairly useless. If you are using the standard version of Outlook then it is tricky to get it to sync, and to get real value from a digital calendar you want it to be available wherever you are, on a phone, tablet or computer.

If you use it with an Exchange account then the Outlook calendar works just fine.

Mac Calendar or iCal

The basic Mac calendar is a great tool for Mac users as long you also have an Apple phone. If you have an Android phone it is difficult to connect the phone and calendars effectively.

As long as you are on all Apple, it is very intuitive for creating appointments, different calendars and managing the usual functions such as creating recurring appointments and setting reminders.

Google Calendar

I love the Google Calendar for its flexibility and ease of use. You can connect it to all your devices, it updates really fast, and by creating multiple calendars you are able to keep things compartmentalised.

Google Calendar also integrates with many other tools so that you can sync across systems.

Google also make it really easy to embed a calendar into a website, so if you want to be able to share your calendar with potential customers then this is a simple and easy way to do so. You can update your events in the calendar and the website will also reflect the changes; minimal effort, maximum results!

Calendar sharing

All the above calendars (excluding Outlook when used without Microsoft Exchange) allow you to share calendars with other people. This means you can share them with colleagues, clients and family to save unnecessary questions about availability and whereabouts. Each tool operates slightly differently but by going to the calendar you want to share and finding the settings or right-clicking, you can send a link to the calendar within a matter of seconds.

Action: Decide if you should be sharing your calendar with collaborators, colleagues or family to make things work smoothly, and share as appropriate.

Default calendars

As well as ensuring that you have a calendar, a system that many small business owners find useful is creating a default calendar. This is like a business timetable which helps you to share your time between all the different jobs a small business owner needs to get done.

One thing that I see over and over again is the boom and bust cycle of small business. You start out all keen bean with no clients, lots of time and you do lots of marketing. Fast forward a few months and the clients are rolling in. You're too busy to do anything but serve your clients and marketing drops off the to-do list. Most people have a natural lifecycle with their clients or products; the clients finish working with you or they're busy and then what? Crickets. So, frantic marketing starts again… a lag period naturally before you get busy but then you're busy again. Too busy to do marketing and so the cycle continues.

The same could be said for dealing with finances, IT, HR and more. We don't prioritise it within our business in the way we should. Big businesses divide their budget up into different departments. Each department is allocated an amount of money to provide services to the corporation in order that it can properly serve its clients. HR looks after staffing, IT manage the systems, Finance makes sure the books balance, the management team look after strategy and the cleaners make sure the place is clean and that there is tea!

Just because you are a one-man band doesn't mean you shouldn't take the corporation approach. Your budget (of time) must be divided up into the different departments that make up your business so that you are best able to serve your customers and you are able to run your business with minimal stress.

Don't forget; you are in charge. You can make up a system that works in a way that makes sense to you so read on with an open mind and ask yourself 'how could I make this work for me?'

How to create a default calendar

First of all, you need to put on your CEO hat. As the leader of your business you need to set a guide for the amount of time that you are going to spend each week, month and year on different activities. You also need to be honest with yourself. If you are having to work four days a week at marketing to get one client who doesn't bring in enough money for a week's wage then you should probably go back and look at your business model. Equally, if you are in the early stages of your business your time will be spent very differently to when you are more established.

With your CEO hat on, think about how much time each week would be reasonable to spend on:

- strategy (planning, goal setting, reviewing reports)

- finance (reconciling accounts, raising invoices, chasing payments, bookkeeping)

- marketing and administration (social media, advertising, networking, speaking, content creation, emails)

- IT (backing up systems, routine maintenance)

- delivery (your actual work and probably the reason you started your business).

You also need to think about how many hours each week you want to work. If you are working a 30-hour week and want to spend 10% of your time on finance you would need to set aside three hours.

You should end up with a list that looks a bit like this:

- Strategy 7% = 2 hours

- Finance 10% = 3 hours

- Marketing and Admin 30% = 9 hours

- IT 3% = 1 hour

- Delivery 50% = 15 hours

So now what?

This is where we create a default calendar, and an online calendar makes this easy. You create a two-hour recurring appointment called 'Strategy' and put it into your working week. Then do the same for Finance and so on until you have a calendar that looks something like this:

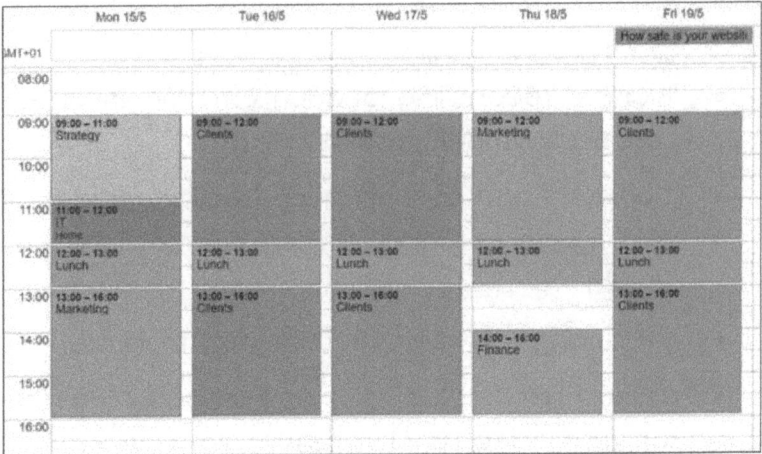

Figure 4: Default calendar containing recurring tasks

If this all feels far too rigid for you then you could try a more lightweight approach. Create small blocks of time that you drop into your calendar every week to give you some space for the basics. Admin, finance and marketing should all be on there. This means that each week you will 'see' those tasks in your calendar and should have some free time to dedicate to them. The balance of effort across all the areas will be more equitable and your business will grow more easily.

A default calendar can be created on paper or online but it is much easier to shift time blocks around with an online calendar.

Action: Download the bonus worksheet 'Create Your Default Calendar' to help you plan this time out (or copy my default one shown in Figure 4 but remember, your business is different to the 'default' so you may need to make tweaks over time).

Booking systems

Once you have your calendar online you can use online systems to enable clients or potential clients to book time with you directly. This saves the back and forth emails that can occur when trying to find a mutually convenient slot, makes you look professional and saves you time.

There are an increasing number of systems that enable you to set up online appointment scheduling and they all share some common features.

- *Create appointment types.* You may have a free 30-minute consultation with new clients as well as 90-minute one-to-one sessions. You need to clearly define the types of appointment you are going to offer online and then create them in the system.

- *Connect to your calendar.* This is where the magic happens. You can define the default times for the appointments you offer. An example might be a free consultation which you could offer on Mondays and Wednesdays. Then you connect to your calendar and the appointment scheduling system checks to see what other commitments you have in your diary and offers times that you are free. Genius eh?

- *Confirm the appointment.* The systems take the email address of the person booking the appointment and sends both them and you confirmation of the appointment. It is also possible to set up reminders, including SMS (text message) reminders to their phone, which can be really useful if people tend to forget to turn up!

- *Payment and booking.* Some systems also allow you to take payment at the point of booking, create booking forms (to collect client information), accept terms and conditions and embed the booking forms into your website for a seamless user experience.

- *Complex appointments.* The most advanced systems allow you to sell packages and then allow the client to book a specific number of time slots. They also allow you to create group classes and sell spaces until the course is full.

What are the options?

Calendly

Calendly offers a really simple interface for offering appointments online and their free package is plenty to get a 30-minute consultation up on your website in a jiffy. Their paid-for package offers more features but doesn't compete with Acuity for features.

Acuity

Acuity is the next step up from Calendly and includes all the fancy features mentioned in the options section. You can take payment, require someone to complete a detailed booking form before they make the appointment and you can also offer group bookings and upsell products related to the session being booked (e.g. a yoga mat to attendees of a yoga class).

Alternatives: Schedule Once, Timetrade, Book me, Book Like a Boss

Action: Decide if you would benefit from an online booking tool.

Time and task management

Time management tools

Developing a system that allows you to allocate your time out in a meaningful way can be a turning point for a small business. Ensuring you allocate time to each of the important (but not always obvious or urgent) areas that need it means your business will grow in a more balanced way.

Once you have the basic plan there are some other tools that you might find useful to make the day last a little bit longer!

Time tracking

If you are a freelance service provider then it is likely that you are charging hourly for your time. In this case it is vital to track your time in a way that easily shows how much time you have spent on each project in order to be able to charge the client correctly.

Knowing how long things take is also important if you charge set prices for work (i.e. a package) to ensure that you are getting paid enough for the work you are doing. If you are a branding consultant charging £995 for a rebrand package, how will you know if this is a fair price if you don't know how long it takes you to deliver the service?

Fortunately, there are a number of tools that will enable you to track your time at the click of a button and neatly drop the information into a spreadsheet. Some accounting tools even integrate a time tracker into their software package so that you can quickly create an invoice based on the time spent and the type of work you were doing.

Toggl and Harvest are cloud-based tools that allow you to click a button to start a session and then click again to stop. You add clients and projects so that you can clearly see how much time you spent where. This can also be shared with the client so that they can see how much they are spending as a project progresses.

If you find yourself getting to the end of the week and wondering where all the time went, then a tool called RescueTime could be deployed to answer that question. RescueTime sits on your computer or phone and tracks the amount of time you spend in each app. It can be a bit of a shock to find out just how much time you are spending on Facebook when you receive your weekly email summary of how productive you were. A great tool to get a picture of how you currently spend your time and to motivate you to do something about it.

If you find that social media is taking over your life then there are apps that will block it. Depending on where you want to block access, you can use Cold Turkey, AppBlocker or BlockApp, for example. These only work for Android as the way Apple lock down their systems makes it impossible to block individual apps. Apple devices now have a built-in tool called Screen Time which allows you to manage your screen time.

Action: Install RescueTime to find out how much time you are wasting each week

and/or

Action: Set up Harvest or Toggl to start tracking the time you allocate to different clients or projects to make sure that you are getting paid enough!

Task management

One thing that all small business owners seem to have in common is that there is more to do than can fit into the day. If this is true for you, then deciding which tasks should take priority each day should be a key activity. Unfortunately there is not much I can do to help you get more than 24 hours in your day but there are some ways of ensuring that you are working on the most important things so that your time is being used really wisely.

If you find yourself frazzled by all the tasks you need to do then the simple act of writing down – whether on paper or digitally – all the things that are popping around in your head can have a very calming effect. Once the 'to-do's' are on paper you can see more clearly what needs doing and start to prioritise.

Simple tools

The back of an envelope has long been used as a to-do list. This system still works brilliantly for people who like a piece of paper and who get enough post that they have spare envelopes lying around! If you are happy with a scrap of paper and your system works for you then I wouldn't recommend you change it.

If, like me, you find that your scrap of paper is often left at home when you get to the supermarket and you are ready to move into the digital age then there are some simple but effective to-do list apps which enable you to have a list across all your devices and add new things and tick off completed ones. You can even share the list with other people; my husband and I share a shopping list so we both know what to get if we find ourselves in the supermarket rather than wishing we could remember what was written on the paper list that's still stuck to the fridge!

What are the options?

There are many to-do list apps out there so have a look in the app stores for something that looks appealing to you. My favourite is Todoist.

If you want to replace simple paper notes with something you can access anywhere, this is a great option. Todoist takes its tasks very seriously. You can organise them into projects, set due dates, add tags and reminders. You can also turn emails into tasks at the click of a button, a brilliant feature for anyone trying to get away from a bulging inbox. Finally, it will integrate with your calendar so you can see what tasks are due each day. A really powerful way to keep on top of all your day-to-day jobs.

As previously mentioned, there are lots of tools on the market that help with to-dos! Most offer a free trial so you can see if they work for you before making a commitment.

Alternatives: Don't Forget the Milk, Wunderlist, Microsoft ToDo, Apple Reminders

Action: If you think an app could help you keep track of things then install a to-do app today!

When does a collection of tasks become a project?

Your to-do list probably consists of lots of tasks that you do regularly: invoicing, paying bills, updating your website, sending blogs, getting the car serviced and buying food. These happen regularly and, while they are part of a bigger picture, they are all standalone tasks.

Sometimes though, we have a collection of tasks that all achieve the same goal and at that point a motley collection of tasks can be renamed as a project. So when does a collection of tasks become a project?

This is a tricky question as it is partly down to individual preference but I would propose that any piece of work that has a beginning, middle and, most importantly, an end, could be a project. Doing general admin is not a project but sending your client Christmas cards could be. Similarly, doing accounting is not a project but sub-mitting your tax return could be. To complete either of these projects you need to complete a series of tasks in a specific order to deliver a defined result. Planning out a project helps to reduce the stress you may have delivering it, helps to manage timescales and costs, and tends to deliver a better result than just getting started and hoping for the best.

When you decide to 'manage' a project, the first step is to define your goal. This needs to be clearly defined so that you know when you have achieved it. 'Getting more customers' is not a goal; running a marketing cam-paign on local radio is.

Once you have defined your goal, you need to write out all the steps that you will need to take to achieve the goal. Make sure you capture every tiny little detail so that you can really understand what you are trying to achieve. Some people find this easiest to do using post-it notes; others just use a big bit of paper and some are happy entering them straight into a project manage-ment tool. There is no right way to do it so get stuck in with whatever feels best for you.

Once you have a list of the tasks that combine to deliver the goal you can start to put them into order, assign them to people to carry out and set due dates. For example, for the radio advertising campaign, you would need to approach the local station to find out prices and dura-tion of adverts before you could make a decision on how long you wanted the advert to be. Once you know how long it is you could work with a script writer to create a compelling advert and then find someone to do the recording and production and so on. Knowing how long different elements will take will help you to create a plan that is achievable, so discussing the usual turnaround time for a radio advert with some producers would help you to plan out your steps in a meaningful way.

Once you have set out all the tasks you can either leave them on post-it notes or the whiteboard, or you can transfer them to some software to enable you to work on them.

The benefit of having a plan on your computer is that you can easily update it, share it with others who are involved and you can integrate it with other tools that you may use.

What are the options?

Spreadsheets

Once again the humble spreadsheet deserves a mention here. Adding all your tasks to a spreadsheet with some due dates and the name of the person responsible for completing the task is a quick and easy way to get your project mapped out. You could even add some conditional formatting to alert you to tasks that are overdue.

The great thing about a spreadsheet is that you can create the rows to contain exactly the information that you want, nothing more, nothing less, and certainly better than nothing!

Once you are ready for a project management tool with a bit more oomph than a spreadsheet, there are some great options available for relatively low cost. In a corporate environment, the favourite is Microsoft Project which sells on the Microsoft site for just under £1,000. Fortunately, there are some much more reasonable alternatives!

Before you start using a project management system it is worth thinking about how your brain works best. If you are a visual person then take a look at Trello; if you like the spreadsheet style of organising, then Asana might work well for you.

Trello

Trello is a card-based system which turns your tasks into a very visual project, looking like post-it notes stuck to a large board. You create a board for your project onto which you can place cards and then cards can hold multiple tasks.

So, for the radio campaign mentioned previously we could have a board for the project, a card for each of the main activities (cost and book radio slots, develop script, hire actors, record adverts, produce adverts) and tasks within the card that are the individual activities that need to be completed to get the whole project completed (i.e. contact radio station for prices, discuss with marketing team, raise purchase order, etc.).

Alternatively, each member of the team can have a card and there can be cards for tasks to be done, underway and completed. This way you can move the tasks from place to place to indicate their status.

You can add notes to tasks as well as due dates and even attach files. This saves you from having to email things back and forth and ensures you are always working from the latest version.

Asana

Asana uses a more traditional approach to display information as text in lines though it has also got a card-based project style if you prefer it. You create milestones which are made up of tasks and sub-tasks until all the details are documented in one place.

You can invite collaborators so everyone you are working with can see how the project is progressing and you can attach files to support the tasks.

The folks at Asana also have a sense of fun; switch on 'celebrations' and you will be rewarded by mythical animals flying across your screen when you have a particularly productive session. I'm not kidding, unicorns are real.

Alternatives: Teamwork, Basecamp and Monday

Action: Decide if project management software could help your business and sign up.

Office tools

Most businesses need to use some form of software for their day-to-day activities. Those of you who have come from an office environment may be familiar with Microsoft Office and the suite of tools that it includes: Word (for writing documents), Excel (spreadsheets for numbers), Outlook (emailing), PowerPoint (presentations) among other tools.

If you are creating invoices, writing reports, trying to keep track of numbers or creating presentations then you are going to need some kind of software to help you do this.

Microsoft is often the first choice of people leaving a corporate environment because they feel they need to have these tools and are familiar with the Office suite, but there are more options which are worth considering.

Microsoft have changed the way that they do business and instead of buying a box with some CDs in to install and owning that software forever, they would like you to buy a subscription to Office 365. Office 365 is a monthly or annual subscription enabling you to use the very latest version of the Office suite. You can choose from a range of levels to ensure that you get the software you need which also includes some cloud storage. A monthly subscription spreads the cost for a new business, which is great but it also means that you are committed to an ongoing cost forever.

If you don't want to use Microsoft products, then take a look at Google. Google is much more than a search engine and it has a totally free set of tools that are arguably better than the Microsoft tools. In order to use them you need to create a Google account, go to Google Drive and then click new. A whole host of programmes will be offered that you can use. These tools are compatible with the Microsoft equivalents so you can create and share documents that everyone can access.

If you have an Apple computer then you also have access to a whole suite of great tools from Apple. These include word processing (Pages), spreadsheets (Numbers) and presentations (Keynote).

If you would rather use something that is a little less integrated with the big software houses, then OpenOffice is a free, open-source tool which offers all the basic functionality you need.

Word processing

Word processing packages such as Microsoft Word, Google Docs, Apache Writer (OpenOffice) and Apple Pages are mainly used for writing documents. As a small business owner you are likely to need at least some of the following:

- letters
- contracts
- invoices and receipts (if you aren't using a finance package that does this for you)
- reports
- eBooks

When you create your documents in any of the above packages, you can use a font that represents your brand, create headers and sections that get your point across clearly, and create templates for documents you use regularly which will save you hours of time in the long run.

Being able to use a simple word processing tool will mean that your communications will always look professional. For those of you who still send physical letters then these tools will enable you to create mail merges where contact data in a spreadsheet can be used to generate a personalised letter for each recipient.

Spreadsheets are cool

I know that just saying the word spreadsheet out loud can bring some people out in a rash but I would urge anyone who wants to be able to track things in their business to give them a chance.

A spreadsheet can be a hardworking team member, enabling you to see the real picture of your business, which in turn will mean you can make better decisions and also reduces the stress of not knowing.

Why are spreadsheets so useful?

Spreadsheets let you collect data together and then analyse it in the same place. You can quickly calculate totals (total profit) or work out averages (average order value, average number of sessions per client) and then generate graphs to show the data in a visual way.

Spreadsheets also let you add conditional formatting. This means that if a cell (one of the boxes of the sheet) meets certain conditions then the box changes colour. The most obvious use for this is to track due dates: when a date is more than three days away the box can be green, within three days it would be yellow and once it is due then red. This turns a page of numbers into something that is easy to interpret. Mainly greens and you are keeping on top of things, mainly reds and you may need some help!

There are several places that you can get hold of a spreadsheet. Microsoft Office has Excel as part of their Office suite (paid-for), Google have a free-to-use version that is easier to understand than Excel and does most of the same things, and Mac users can use Numbers which is intuitive to use and free to iOS users.

Whichever spreadsheet you decide to use there will be pre-made templates that can give you a feel for the capabilities. These include budgeting, planning, schedules and lots more.

The most useful things that a spreadsheet can do (which I suggest you learn) include:

- Mathematical functions like adding up columns, averaging, working out percentages. All without you needing a calculator!

- Conditional formatting. Changing the look of a cell dependant on the value within it means that sheets of meaningless numbers can be colour coded, instantly turning them into an understandable, visual resource.

- Charts. Sometimes a sheet of numbers, even with conditional formatting, doesn't show what's happening. A chart can be easily generated to enable you to track progress or work out the different percentages of sales type and much more.

Presentations

Some businesses need to share information visually, either for speaking, networking, client pitches or just for information. This is usually done by creating a digital presentation. The Microsoft Office tool that does this is called PowerPoint and sometimes a slide deck is referred to as a PowerPoint.

The great thing about these slide packages is that they let you create more engaging presentations so that people can get the key messages you are trying to share. The traditional slide consists of a title with some bullet points below, but you can do much more with slides now.

Start by branding the slides. Find the Master slide which acts as a template for all the other slides you create and add your logo, and set the colours and fonts to match your business branding.

Once you start creating slides you don't have to stick to just text. It is possible to embed images, video and audio into a presentation so don't restrict yourself. If you are using video and audio make sure that the files are stored on the computer that the presentation will be delivered from.

You can also animate the presentation. This means that the different items on the page appear when you click the mouse button. Used carefully this can be a useful way of keeping your audience focused on what you are talking about rather than skipping ahead through the slides to what's up next. Used too much it can give the audience motion sickness, so be sparing with animation!

If you are regularly presenting it is worth getting hold of a clicker which plugs into the computer and allows you to scroll through the slides without having to be next to the computer. This means you can stand up and engage with your audience, rather than having to stay next to the PC.

There are a few options that you can look at for creating slides.

What are the options?

Microsoft PowerPoint

Microsoft PowerPoint comes with the Office package and does pretty much everything you could need. It is a paid-for tool though, so if you are looking for something free read on.

Google Slides

Google Slides is the Google alternative to PowerPoint. It is easy to use and a good option if you are on a budget, but it does require an internet connection to run, making it a bit of a risk for a big event.

Keynote

Apple make Keynote free to anyone with an iCloud account and if you have a Mac computer you can download a version to your device so that it can be used without an internet connection.

Prezi

PowerPoint, Slides and Keynote are pretty similar in terms of functions so the one you use will come down to personal preference. If you are looking for something a little different then Prezi offers a new and exciting way of creating a presentation.

Unlike the other three tools, Prezi imagines your presentation as one massive picture and the 'slides' allow you to zoom in to look at particular elements in detail. This is hard to explain in words so I suggest you take a look at some of their demo presentations on their website to see if it could work for you.

Action: Decide which tools will be useful for your business. Sign up for the accounts and set up templates so you are ready when they are needed.

Cool tools

The following tools don't fit particularly well into any other section but are too brilliant not to mention.

Make some space in your brain! Use a note tool

With so much information available to us, it is little wonder that we can become overwhelmed, and while much of what we read and watch is not that useful, being able to quickly access the information that *is* relevant saves time and stress.

There are some amazing information storage tools available which let you gather information in different formats – text, audio, image, files, videos- into one place and categorise them with groups and tags.

This means that you can find them again when you need them rather than spending time Googling to see if you can relocate the article that you were sure you read on-line but which turns out to have been in a magazine!

These tools use cloud storage to store your notes on a server that can be accessed by any device you chose to connect from, meaning your information is available wherever you are in the world as long as you have an internet connection.

Sounds good? Let's look at the options.

Evernote

I am a self-confessed Evernote fan. Started as a simple note-taking app, you create notes which can be stored in notebooks. It sounds simple but the addition of tags and in-note searching makes Evernote really powerful. It also has a web clipper which allows you to turn any web page into a note at the click of a button and you can do the same with emails if you add an extension to your email client.

Microsoft OneNote

With similar functionality to Evernote, this tool is included in the Office 365 subscription and allows you to create virtual notes from all your devices.

Make your business beautiful: design tools

We all know that a nicely designed piece of marketing will catch people's attention much faster than something bland or badly designed. Until recently, unless you had a handy family member who was a designer, the only way to get professional-looking designs was to pay a designer to create your flyers, leaflets and other marketing materials.

With the advent of online software tools this is all changing. You can now access powerful design software, hosted entirely online, and create your own gorgeous designs. And this can all be done really quickly.

Caveat: There is no substitute for a great graphic designer. Once you have the resources I would really recommend having a branding exercise done with a professional who can build a whole brand for you.

There are a number of great design tools out there, but for the small business owner there are two which earn the top spot time and time again.

Canva

Canva offers a fee account and lots of amazing templates to help you get started with creating designs for just about anything. These include social media posts, flyers, documents and much more. It also allows you to access free stock photos and lots of icons and elements to make your designs stand out. Some of the images require a payment, and you can opt to pay $1 per item or a monthly all-inclusive fee. Fantastic for creating marketing materials for your business.

PicMonkey

PicMonkey lets you edit photos as well as create designs, a bit like a lightweight version of Photoshop. It doesn't have as many templates as Canva so is better if you know what you want to create or need to edit photos, but it has more editing functions to get your photos looking perfect.

Capturing information: surveys and feedback

However you work with people, whatever service or product you sell, proof of how good it is from real-life people is invaluable. Testimonials act as proof that people value your services and will help to form a trusting relationship. They are a great way of blowing your own trumpet without having to do it yourself, but asking for them and getting people to respond to your requests can be a bit of a challenge. One way to make this process easier for both your client/customers and yourself is to create a feedback form which can be completed online and which you send a link to for the customer to complete.

This works equally well for one-to-one clients, group feedback following workshops or lessons or at the bottom of an order confirmation if you are selling a product. You may wish to add an incentive, depending on your business, for completion. This could be anything from a discount code for a future purchase, to entry into a monthly prize draw, to a free download of a bonus training session.

As well as capturing testimonials, survey tools can also be used if you are trying to understand what your customers might be interested in buying in the future, before creating new courses, or stocking new lines – an online survey does the job beautifully.

The same survey tools can also help to speed up new client applications by capturing their information before you first speak, making the conversations you have more valuable as you are able to get straight to the key points. If you are in health or therapeutic fields then the medical forms can all be completed online to save you from having to re-enter data.

What do these tools actually do?

There are typically two parts to the survey system: the front end that the customer enters the information into, and a back end which is where the form is created and the data from all the forms is collated into a single spreadsheet.

Before you start to create a form, think about the type of questions you might want to use. Typically you can ask:

- open questions in both short and longer text boxes
- yes or no questions
- multiple-choice questions (which can either be one or many answers)
- scales of opinion (such as between 1 and 10 or very unlikely to very likely).

You can also use the forms to capture email addresses and phone numbers if appropriate and the form will require the email address to have the correct configuration.

Think carefully about the information you would like to be able to pull out of the survey. For example, if you have a survey for feedback from a workshop or a product sale you could ask:

> 'How likely are you to recommend this
> (fill in the blank) to a friend or colleague?'

If you have a scale of very unlikely, unlikely, not sure, quite likely, very likely, then assuming the majority of people are happy they will probably answer one of the positive choices, and you could then make a statement based on the actual numbers such as '95% of attendees of this workshop would recommend it to a colleague'. This is much more powerful marketing material than one person saying it was good, especially if it is combined with the numbers of people who attended.

Once you have your questions ready you need to decide which tool to use.

What are the options?

Google Forms

The good old Google gang didn't stop at word processing and spreadsheets; they created some gorgeous forms which are 'drag and drop' meaning you can move the questions around the screen till they are in the right order. The form sits in your Google Drive so you do need to have a (free) Google account to use this, and you can share the form once you have completed it by sharing the special link that the form creates. Once the data is entered and the form submitted, the data is added as a new row to a spreadsheet in Google Sheets. Genius. No typing in data, and it is already in a spreadsheet for you to start your analysis so that you can create some great marketing statements or work out how many people would prefer a smaller-size cake range vs a larger one.

Typeform

Typeform offers a great freemium product which makes some lovely forms. These are more professional looking than Google's offering but do come with the Typeform branding in the free version. Typeform offers a few other advantages over Google Forms, one of which is the ability to embed the form into a website. This means that people can complete a survey on your website, without having to leave; many of them won't even realise that you were using a different tool.

Once completed, the data from the forms is automatically shown within Typeform and can also be exported to a spreadsheet. The free plan offers unlimited responses and questions and the paid-for versions allow you to get clever with logic so that questions are tailored based on answers that have already been given as well as calculating scores so that you could use it to create quizzes.

SurveyMonkey

SurveyMonkey deserves a mention on this list as for a long time it was the best survey tool available, but as the free version restricts the ability to download the results I would only recommend it if you are happy to pay for the premium version and if you are not keen on Typeform.

Tech ninja section: connecting systems together

So far we have covered some great systems. Really great systems. They do some good stuff that really can help with getting things done. And yet, you find yourself thinking I wish that when someone bought something on PayPal they were automatically added to my email list in Mailchimp. Or I wish that I didn't have to think about backing up my email subscribers. Why don't these systems all talk to each other?!?

Well fear not. While there are lots of systems that can be forced to talk to each other using APIs (Application Programming Interface) for which you need a proper tech geek, there are also some apps that work to connect different bits of software and automatically make things happen.

Think of these as a translator which works between two systems, explaining what one is trying to say to the other one which is talking in a whole different language. Because the interpreter has limited vocabulary, the things that you can get the systems to do is limited to the words they know, but they can still do lots of useful things.

Zapier

Zapier is the current integration app of choice and you can get started with a free account that gives you a feel for what it can achieve. I pronounce it Zapier which rhymes with happier, as it definitely makes me happier!

You start off by creating an account and then you need to choose the two apps that you want to connect together. Start with something simple like adding all photos that you are tagged in on Facebook into a Dropbox folder. This means you need to authorise Zapier to access both accounts.

If you change your mind you can revoke access at any time by going into the settings of the apps that you authorised Zapier to use.

Choose the account that you want the trigger to start with. In this example it's Facebook, and you will be presented with a range of possible things that can 'trigger' the zap (or connection between the two systems). You then choose whether you want a filter. This means whether you want the integration to trigger every time the trigger occurs or only sometimes. This is useful if you are triggering a zap for a PayPal purchase but only want it to work if a specific product is purchased. You then choose the second app of the zap and authorise that. Then you choose the end action: save to Dropbox where you can also specify the folder. Finally you set the zap to live and from there on any time you are tagged in a photo it will be saved. Bingo!

This is a basic example but there are some more to get you thinking:

- add PayPal purchasers to your accounting system and create an invoice
- add webinar attendees to your email marketing list
- add event attendees to a spreadsheet
- move people from a sub-list of your email marketing onto your main list after a welcome sequence
- create a spreadsheet of people who share your content on social media
- create tweets from a specific category of note
- receive a text whenever you get an email from a particular person or with a specific title.

I could go on. The best way to start understanding Zapier and its potential is to have a go.

Action: Create a Zapier account and have a play around with the functions.

Keep it safe...

Passwords are a bit of a nightmare for all computer users. The more accounts we get the more passwords we get, and we are meant to have a different one for every account. Unless you have a Mensa-worthy IQ or a photographic memory you are going to start forgetting passwords pretty quickly.

Here's a scary fact for you: if you reset a password once a week then you are spending four hours a year resetting your passwords. That's a working week each decade. On resetting passwords. Surely there are better things to do with your day?

What can you do?

Password managers are the answer to this dilemma. These are online tools that you have just one password for and then behind that they remember all the passwords for each account you have.

Before we get too far down this route it's worth addressing security. Consider the different accounts you hold and think about the worst-case scenario of those accounts being hacked. In most cases it would be embarrassing but not the end of the world. Most of the accounts that hold sensitive data offer two-factor authentication (where you also have to enter a code sent to you via text, or a widget for banks), which means that even with the password your account is still safe. I recommend switching on two-factor authentication for any account that holds sensitive data so you can use the password manager more securely.

In summary

Password managers use a master password (which you do need to be able to remember) to store all your other passwords. Once you are logged into the password manager it will autofill all the login fields for your other tools.

There is a risk that the account could be compromised, along with all your logon details, if the password manager is ever hacked into. However, the password management companies spend all their time trying to prevent this from happening, and are probably more vigilant that we could ever be.

Use a password manager that offers encryption, meaning that your details are stored in a nonsensical state on their servers and only decrypted by people who have the key (you!). Switch on two-factor authentication to ensure maximum security.

The password manager will remember all your passwords even if your bag gets stolen with the notebook that you write all your account details in.

The password manager will generate complex passwords for you that are much harder to hack into than the usual human-generated passwords.

Some of the password apps also have a mobile version which syncs across your devices so that wherever you are, you can log in at the touch of a button, saving yourself half a day a year!

Some of the password managers also let you share login details with other people from the app. This means they don't need to see the details, which makes it a safer way of sharing.

What are the options?

LastPass

LastPass offers all the functionality you need from a password manager with lots of scope for configuration. It has a great free version and should you want the paid version, it is very reasonably priced.

Keychain

Keychain is the default package on all Apple computers and does most of the things mentioned above. It doesn't have a master password separate to your Apple account though, so be aware that if you hand over your computer or phone to someone else they potentially have access to all your passwords. LastPass lets you choose whether you need to enter the password every time you log in so is more secure in this way. It doesn't offer the ability to share passwords securely with other parties, so may not be ideal if this is a requirement.

Alternatives: Dashlane, Someone, StickyPassword

Action: Decide if a password tool would make your business run better.

Chapter 4 checklist

The checklists are designed to help you decide what you need to do in your business. Not all activities are relevant to all businesses so choose those that are applicable and identify whether the activity is something to do now or in the future. As this chapter covers lots of tools there are lots of actions listed but don't feel you need to implement all of them!

Action	Not relevant	For the future	To do now	Done it!
Register with HMRC.				
Obtain necessary insurance cover.				
Check whether you are required to register with the Information Commissioner's Office (https://ico.org.uk/).				
Decide if you are going to manage your bookkeeping yourself or outsource it.				
Ensure you have registered with the relevant tax authorities and got your login details in a safe place.				
Decide whether you are going to engage an accountant to do your tax return or do it yourself. Find an accountant if necessary.				
Decide how you are going to keep a record of your accounts. Sign up for your chosen software or set up a spreadsheet.				
Decide whether you are going to open a business bank account and research the best account for you. Open your account.				

Choose a method of taking card payments in person if this is relevant to your business.				
Make sure you have a separate business and personal PayPal account.				
Create a Stripe account if you want to be able to take payments via 3rd-party software at a lower fee than PayPal.				
Decide whether to physically back up your data. Obtain the necessary hard drives and diarise a regular backup.				
Decide whether to use cloud storage and which provider. Set up and ensure all your business-critical data is backed up to the cloud.				
Check you have antivirus installed and install if not.				
Consider using a malware scanner to increase your security.				
Commit to switch off your computer/phone/ other device daily.				

Book a service if your computer is more than a couple of years old and running slowly.				
Check the speed of your connection. If it's slow check with your provider whether you could get a faster connection and the costs involved.				
Decide on a domain name and purchase.				
Set up email at your domain, connect to your preferred email client and add a signature.				
Create an inbox management system that works for you. Commit to keeping your inbox clear.				
Decide if you should be sharing your calendar with collaborators, colleagues or family to make things work smoothly, and share as appropriate.				
Download the bonus worksheet 'Create Your Default Calendar' to help you plan your time.				
Decide if you would benefit from an online booking tool.				

Install RescueTime to find out how much time you are wasting each week.				
Set up Harvest or Toggl to start tracking the time you allocate to different clients or projects to make sure that you are getting paid enough.				
If you think an app could help you keep track of things then install a to-do app today.				
Decide if project management software could help your business and sign up.				
Decide which tools will be useful for your business. Sign up for the accounts and set up templates so you are ready when they are needed.				
Decide whether any of the following 'cool tools' would be useful for your business:				
Notetaking tool				
Design tool				
Survey tool				
Integration tool				
Password management				

Chapter 5

Bringing it all together

This book has given you a whistle-stop tour of all the main types of tool that you could be using in a small business. In this final section I will discuss what to do if the tool you need is not covered, and then we'll take a look at how to bring together all the action points that have been mentioned into a manageable plan for your business systems.

Choosing a new tool

It's not possible to summarise all the options for every tool that you might want to use in your business; technology moves so fast and businesses change their offers frequently. By the time you read this it is possible that some of the tools I mention are no longer in existence. But don't worry! You can still make informed choices about what is out there.

What I have tried to do is list all the functions that every software family could do so that you can pick the ones that would benefit your business. Remember YOU are the expert on your business.

When a big business chooses new software they usually go through a rigorous process to find the right product for their needs and there are some useful steps that we can borrow and apply to a small business when we need a job done.

There are two ways you can approach choosing new software.

Requirements definition

1.   Write out your requirements. What do you want to get done? What are the features that the system should have? Some features might sound really cool (e.g. having unicorns that fly across the screen from time to time!) but don't really deliver any useful value, whereas other features are deal breakers (e.g. being able to accept payments via Stripe).

2.   Once you have a list of requirements then categorise the requirements into 'Essential' (you won't use something that doesn't have this), 'Nice to have' (this would be good to have but you could work without it) and 'Extras' (the heated seats of the software world. You don't need them but they add to your enjoyment of the system).

3.   Finally, compare the available systems against your list. If you want to be fancy you can use a points system. Discard any systems that don't meet all the 'Essential' requirements. Then give two points for everything in the 'Nice to have' section and one point for everything in the 'Extras' section.

- Add up your points and you should have a winner! If the winner by the points method isn't the one you want to use, at least you have clarified that you have a favourite.

- Choosing a system like this enables you to separate the shiny sales promises from the reality of what a system can do and gets to the detail of the different tools.

The 'suck it and see' method

This is the complete opposite to the previous technique! With so many companies offering free trials of their software you can run live comparisons of similar tools. This enables you to pick your favourite based on real experience.

This method is best used for things that don't take ages to set up and/or learn the basics for as you would be discarding all that work if the system is no good. However, it is a good way to compare systems for things that are quick to set up such as note-taking apps or presentation software.

Think of three tasks that you would expect to do in the tool and do them in each of the systems. Contact the support team for each business and ask the same question. Compare the responses not just in terms of the answer but how quickly they respond and how they made you feel. Often the differences in software products are most clearly seen when something doesn't work and the support is critical in getting you working again!

A final plea: keep the big picture in mind at all times. Remember, you know best. Get the information you need to make the right decisions and good luck!

Creating your action plan

As we have worked through the book, if you have been using the checklists at the end of each chapter, you will have picked up a number of actions that you feel could benefit your business.

It would be very easy to tick a few off and carry on with your day-to-day business and not take the action to make your business work better. But that's not what I want for your business, and if you want to make the changes needed to get things running like clockwork, then please take up my SORTED challenge.

Download the checklists (if you haven't already) found at www.alicejennings.co.uk/book-bonuses and work through the actions that are listed. Mark each as 'not relevant', 'for the future', 'to do now' or 'done'.

Decide how much time you can dedicate each week to getting your business systems in order.

Using the Monthly Worksheet (also available from the book downloads at www.alicejennings.co.uk/book-bonuses), enter some actions from the high-priority tasks, ensuring that the estimated time taken will roughly match the amount of time you have available. Set aside the time in your calendar (online or otherwise) to ensure that you are able to complete the tasks.

At this point you can continue scheduling in all your 'to-do now' and 'for the future' actions into the annual planner to give you a plan for the year. Alternatively you can work a month at a time and complete a new sheet once the first is finished. Think about how you work best. Do longer-term goals make you feel secure or constrained? Will seeing all the tasks feel overwhelming whereas a shorter timescale will be more manageable?

Make plans that suit you and your business. And last but not least, come over to my Facebook Group SORTED (www.alicejennings.co.uk/sorted) and join the discussions around the best systems and tools for small business.